"Then Zorn Said to Largent..."

The Best Seattle Seahawks Stories Ever Told

Chris Cluff, Paul Moyer, and Dave Wyman

TRIUMPH
BOOKS

Copyright © 2008 by Chris Cluff, Paul Moyer, and Dave Wyman

No part of this publication may be reproduced, stored in a retrieval system, or transmitted, in any form by any means, electronic, mechanical, photocopying, or otherwise, without the prior written permission of the publisher, Triumph Books, 542 S. Dearborn St., Suite 750, Chicago, Illinois 60605.

Triumph Books and colophon are registered trademarks of Random House, Inc.

Library of Congress Cataloging-in-Publication Data

Cluff, Chris, 1970–
 Then Zorn said to Largent— : the best Seattle Seahawks stories ever told / Chris Cluff, Paul Moyer, and Dave Wyman.
     p. cm.
   ISBN-13: 978-1-60078-132-2
   ISBN-10: 1-60078-132-2
 1. Seattle Seahawks (Football team) I. Moyer, Paul, 1961– II. Wyman, Dave, 1964– III. Title.
   GV956.S4C484 2008
   796.332'6409797772—dc22
                                     2008022367

This book is available in quantity at special discounts for your group or organization. For further information, contact:

Triumph Books
542 South Dearborn Street
Suite 750
Chicago, Illinois 60605
(312) 939-3330
Fax (312) 663-3557

Printed in U.S.A.
ISBN: 978-1-60078-132-2
Design by Patricia Frey
Editorial production by Prologue Publishing Services, LLC
All photos courtesy of Getty Images unless otherwise indicated.

table of contents

Introduction	vii
Chapter 1: The Early Days	**1**
Birth of the Seahawks	3
The Zorn Identity	5
Patera Strikes Out	7
Chapter 2: Ground Chuck	**9**
In 1983 Chuck Taught Our Team to Believe	11
In 1984 We Lost Warner but Not Our Drive	17
Chuck Knox	21
Curt Warner	29
Chapter 3: 1987	**39**
The Strike	41
Kenny Easley	47
The Boz	52
Chapter 4: 1988	**57**
The First Division Title	59
Ken Behring	65
Chapter 5: The Quarterbacks	**71**
Dave Krieg	73
First-Round Flops	78
Chapter 6: Teammates	**85**
Tez	87
Secondary Stories	90

Jacob, Joe, and Jeff	**95**
Freelancin' Freddie	**97**
Soft Body, Softer Hands	**98**
Fenner's Rep	**99**
Gaines-ville and Butts	**100**
Rufe, Rufe, Rufe!	**102**
Blades Runner	**105**
Paul Skansi: The Human Target	**105**
Bad Citizen Kane	**106**
Lifesaving Missed Tackle	**107**
"Do I Hypnotize You with My Eyes?"	**107**
Bevo Did What It Took	**108**
Fightin' Feasel	**108**
"If You're Scared, Say You're Scared"	**109**
Nervous? Or Just a BSer?	**109**
Chapter 7: Tough Guys	**111**
Moyer's Manhood	**113**
Heck of an Uppercut	**115**
A Ballsy Strategy	**115**
The Best Fight I Ever Saw	**116**
How Catlin Handled Chaos	**118**
Toe Shots	**119**
Chapter 8: Assistants	**121**
TomCat	**123**
The Other Assistants	**126**
Chapter 9: Seasonal Stories	**137**
In 1986 We Bombed Out	**139**
In 1989 a Grudge Match	**139**
In 1990 We Waved a White Flag	**140**
In 1992 Our Offense Was Offensive	**143**
In 1994 We Were Finished When Frier Was Paralyzed	**144**

Chapter 10: The Holmgren Era	**147**
Holmgren's Teams	**149**
The Coach and the Quarterback	**151**
The Polarizing Running Back	**153**
"He's Just a Guard"	**157**
Character and Characters	**159**
Chapter 11: Numbers Games	**161**
Weigh-In Day	**163**
Money Matters	**165**
Chapter 12: Game Day	**169**
The Blue Thunder Dome	**171**
Oh, Crap!	**174**
Turf Talk	**176**
Favorite Foes	**179**
Chapter 13: Down Time	**181**
Guns 'n' Poses	**183**
There and Back Again	**184**
Howard's Place	**185**
Silk Stalker	**186**
Chapter 14: Seattle's Best	**187**
All-Time Teams	**189**
Ring of Honor	**194**

introduction

The Seattle Seahawks have been a study in contrast for more than three decades. They have gone from lovable underdogs in the 1970s to playoff contenders in the 1980s to less-lovable losers in the 1990s to the Super Bowl contenders they are today. It has been a roller-coaster ride full of highs and lows, with good guys and not-so-good guys, great moments and horrible ones, happy times and sad.

Paul Moyer has been associated with the team as a player, coach, or broadcaster for 25 years; Dave Wyman was a Seahawk during the team's first heyday in the 1980s and is a radio analyst of the current team. Together in this compilation, they reminisce about some of the best and worst moments in team history, along with many of the players and coaches who have populated the franchise over the past 32 years.

Paul and Dave will re-introduce you to some of the team's most popular (or infamous) figures—Chuck Knox, Dave Krieg, Curt Warner, Kenny Easley, Brian Bosworth, Cortez Kennedy, and others—and share stories that give you insights into the personalities of many of their former teammates. Some of them are studies in contrast themselves.

Paul and Dave also will take you behind the scenes at team headquarters, where you will learn how players dreaded paydays and went through preposterous rituals to make weight on weigh-in days, and where you will raise your eyebrows over a particular incident that took place in the training room. And then they will let you join them on game days, showing you just how tough and mean players needed to be to play in the NFL.

Paul will take you on a guided tour through the 1983 and 1984 seasons, when Knox first turned the Seahawks into a playoff team and Super Bowl contender. And Paul and Dave will revisit the 1987 players strike, giving you two slightly different views on the season that forever changed the NFL and the relationships between teammates, owners, and fans.

They will relive the 1988 season, in which they helped the Seahawks win their first division title under the new ownership of Ken Behring. And they will talk about how the team changed in the seasons following and sank from a classy, businesslike franchise under the Nordstroms to something quite different under Behring.

By the end of it, you'll have gotten a first-person glimpse at the team's rise in the 1980s and fall in the 1990s, and gotten the former players' look at its rebirth under Mike Holmgren.

So sit back and enjoy *"Then Zorn Said to Largent..."*—a first-person collection of some of the best stories in the history of the Seattle Seahawks...

chapter 1
The Early Days

The late, great Kingdome was home to not only Seattle's Seahawks, but the Mariners from MLB and the SuperSonics from the NBA, as well.
Courtesy AP/Wide World Photos

Birth of the Seahawks

When the Seahawks played their first game—an exhibition at the Kingdome against the San Francisco 49ers on August 1, 1976—it was the culmination of a four-year quest to bring an NFL franchise to Seattle.

The genesis for pro football in Seattle came from Northwest businessmen Herman Sarkowsky and Ned Skinner.

Sarkowsky was a national figure in thoroughbred racing and one of Seattle's most successful real estate developers; Skinner was a Seattle shipping magnate and one of the first owners of the Space Needle.

Sarkowsky had cofounded the Portland Trail Blazers of the NBA in 1970, and soon after that he and Skinner began talking about bringing an NFL franchise to the Northwest. They formed Seattle Professional Football in 1972 in an effort to lobby for an expansion club. And two years later, their efforts paid off as the NFL awarded Seattle a franchise, even though Sarkowsky and Skinner had not yet put together a complete ownership group.

The league actually began to interview other prospective groups, and Sarkowsky and Skinner recruited four other prominent Seattle businessmen to their group. Lloyd Nordstrom was the last of the partners to sign on, but once he got there, he agreed to become the majority owner by paying 51 percent of the $16 million franchise fee. And that sealed the deal for the NFL.

The league awarded the franchise to Seattle in June 1974 and approved the Nordstrom-led ownership group six months later. The group also included Howard Wright, Lamont Bean, and Lynn Himmelman.

Sarkowsky led the search for a general manager and landed on John Thompson, who had been the executive director of the NFL Management Council. Thompson was hired in March 1975, and in June 1975 the group chose "Seahawks" as the team name from among 20,365 entries (151 suggested Seahawks).

Sarkowsky and Thompson then began to look for a coach. They decided on Minnesota defensive line coach Jack Patera over

Marv Levy, Leeman Bennett, and Monte Clark. Levy had turned the Montreal Alouettes into one of the Canadian Football League's best teams. Bennett was coaching receivers for the Los Angeles Rams, who happened to be run by future Seahawks coach Chuck Knox, and Clark was in charge of the Miami Dolphins' offense. All three would be head coaches in the NFL within the next two years, but Sarkowsky fell in love with Patera.

"John and I flew to Minnesota and interviewed Jack," Sarkowsky said in a 1979 interview. "We had interviewed all the others twice, but this was our first talk with Jack. There was something about him. Afterwards, I said, 'That's our guy.' Of all the people we interviewed, my reaction was that that's the guy we want. John agreed."

Sarkowsky said Patera had all of the qualities he was looking for in the coach of an expansion team.

"The way he answered questions, his philosophy about the game," Sarkowsky said, "stability, a tendency not to get overemotional—which I think is important when you're dealing with a lot of young people of questionable talent the first couple of years—leadership qualities, the ability to make good staff decisions, and a certain charisma was apparent to us."

Patera certainly had the résumé for the job. He had coached two of the most talented defensive lines in NFL history—the Los Angeles Rams' Fearsome Foursome and the Minnesota Vikings' Purple People Eaters.

It also probably did not hurt that Patera had Northwest roots. He had grown up in Portland, Oregon, and attended the University of Oregon.

So, four years after Sarkowsky and Skinner had conceived the idea, Seattle had its football team and the men who would run it.

Tragically, however, the majority owner never got to see it in action. Lloyd Nordstrom died of a heart attack while vacationing in Mexico on January 20, 1976—just 17 days after Patera had been hired and less than seven months before the Seahawks were to play their first game.

The Zorn Identity

The Seahawks were assembled in the usual expansionist way, cobbled together with other teams' castoffs and a bunch of young players acquired through the draft. Like most expansion teams, they weren't very talented.

Patera tried to use his own brand of discipline to turn them into a cohesive unit. Among his tactics, he refused to allow water during 90-degree practices at training camp in Cheney, Washington; he didn't allow players to sit on their helmets during practice; he required them all to wear business attire when on road trips; he forbade fraternization with opposing team members. He made it clear that everyone was replaceable.

That was the old-school disciplinarian. Then there was the new-age strategist who ran an offense unlike the NFL had ever seen—one that seemed to have all of the discipline of a three-ring circus.

It was one of the most innovative offenses of that era, and it was run by a spindly, undrafted left-handed quarterback out of Cal Poly-Pomona named Jim Zorn. His favorite target was another castoff, a wide receiver the Houston Oilers shipped to Seattle for an eighth-round draft pick just before the 1976 season started. His name, of course, was Steve Largent.

Because the Seahawks weren't very talented, Patera felt he needed to be creative. It worked. Zorn and Largent soon had the league taking notice of the Seahawks' unpredictable offense, which featured plenty of trick plays and unusual tactics.

"Most of what we did was by design and scripted," Zorn said years later. "For us it was lots of bootleg. It was sprint-outs. We had the sprint draw with [running back] Sherman Smith. I would sprint out. I scrambled. With us, we had a very wide-open offense when it came to the AFC West.

"We were one of the first teams to put three receivers on the field and put people in motion. I remember Kansas City went the other way. They put three running backs on the field and tried to cram it down your throat. We had a different approach."

Although the Seahawks won only two games in their first year—including an ugly one against fellow expansion team Tampa Bay—they quickly became a team to contend with.

"We were a struggling franchise, yet we had some very interesting talent," Largent said. "We actually did exceedingly better than people anticipated us doing from year one."

In 1976 Zorn set a rookie record for passing yards (2,571) and led the NFL in attempts (439). Those numbers earned him the honor of NFC Offensive Rookie of the Year.

By 1978—their third season—the Seahawks had become a winning team. Zorn threw for more than 3,000 yards, and Largent surpassed 1,000 receiving yards for the first time as the Hawks swept the Oakland Raiders and finished 9–7 in the league's first 16-game season. Patera was named NFL Coach of the Year, and Thompson was Executive of the Year.

"Jimmy had a knack for scrambling, and we were never dead," said former linebacker Keith Butler, who was drafted in the second round in 1978. "So many things could happen. He would end up making a lot of plays because of his feet and Steve Largent getting open. We could never be counted out. The defense started catching up with the offense, and we became a pretty good team. But the reason we were 9–7 was because of our offense."

The Hawks rebounded from a 1–5 start to win eight of their last 11 games in 1979. After a slow start, the offense picked it up and was at its creative best, particularly when the Seahawks made their first appearance on *Monday Night Football*. In one of the most fabled plays in franchise history, Zorn hit kicker Efren Herrera with a pass on a fake field goal for a first down that helped the Seahawks rally from a 14–0 deficit to beat the Atlanta Falcons 31–28.

But once again, 9–7 was not good enough to get the Seahawks into the playoffs. Then, as the schedule got tougher and injuries hit, they sank to 4–12 in 1980. After a 4–3 start, they lost their final nine games that year.

Patera let the players know that was not acceptable.

"Jack was a straightforward guy," Butler said. "He didn't mince words. Our facility was down on Lake Washington back then, and we were practicing before one game in December, and Jack called everyone together.

"He said, 'Now, men, take a look around you.' And he started talking about how beautiful it was around us, pointing out the Cascade Mountains to the east and the Olympics to the west, pristine Lake Washington and the beautiful skyline of Seattle. 'Now, there's a lot worse places to play in the NFL,' he said. 'So if you like what you see, you'd better start playing, or you won't be here.'

"That showed us it was a business."

Something Zorn and Patera found out firsthand soon after that.

Patera Strikes Out

The Seahawks continued to struggle in 1981, going 6–10. That led Patera to bench Zorn and put in another unheralded quarterback, an undrafted second-year player from soon-to-be-defunct Milton College named Dave Krieg.

Krieg started the first two games of 1982—both of which ended in losses—and then the season was shut down by a players' strike. That was when the Nordstroms decided to fire Patera and Thompson.

The coach and GM had drawn the players' wrath when they had waived starting receiver Sam McCullum before the season. McCullum was one of the most popular players on the team, and his teammates accused Patera and Thompson of cutting him because he was the team's union representative. The release of McCullum had created a public backlash by union supporters against the Nordstrom department store chain. On top of that, Patera had been arrested for drunken driving the week before the strike.

So there were a lot of reasons for the Nordstroms to be unhappy, but they insisted the firing was completely based on the team's record—the Seahawks had gone 10–24 over the past two-plus seasons and were 35–57 in six-plus years under Patera and Thompson.

"We have been disappointed at our lack of progress on the football field, and that is the sole reason for the dismissal," Elmer Nordstrom told reporters on October 14, 1982. "It became apparent in our early-season performance that things hadn't turned around."

When the strike ended eight weeks later, Mike McCormack, the team's director of football operations, who was doubling as interim coach, reinstated Zorn as the starting quarterback. The Seahawks won four of the final seven games, finishing the disrupted season with a 4–5 record and failing to qualify for the AFC's eight-team, loser-out postseason tournament.

"It was really unfortunate what the Seahawks did with that strike," Largent said. "It took us a while to recover. That was a little unsettling for everybody. When you lose a coach, it's not an easy thing."

It turned out for the better, though, as the Seahawks hired Chuck Knox and turned into one of the AFC's top teams for the next decade.

Zorn's days as the team's star ended halfway through the 1983 season, when Krieg replaced him for good and led the Seahawks to the playoffs.

Zorn never quarterbacked a playoff team himself, but he always gave the fans a great show and was perhaps the most entertaining quarterback in team history. He started 100 games for the Seahawks and finished with 20,122 passing yards, 107 touchdowns, and 133 interceptions in nine seasons with the team.

Zorn was let go by the Seahawks after the 1984 season and finished his career with backup stints in Green Bay (1985) and Tampa Bay (1987) before embarking on a coaching career that brought him back to Seattle twice and culminated with a position as head coach of the Washington Redskins in 2008.

Largent, meanwhile, went on to become the Seahawks' first homegrown Hall of Famer while helping the team go to the playoffs four times in the 1980s with Krieg at quarterback and Knox as coach.

chapter 2
Ground Chuck

Chuck Knox instilled toughness and a winning attitude in the franchise during his tenure in Seattle.

In 1983 Chuck Taught Our Team to Believe

(by Paul Moyer)

When Chuck Knox was hired to coach the Seahawks in 1983, we had a nucleus that was very talented. He knew the one ingredient that was missing was a team that believed in itself. He was trying to instill a winning attitude. So he brought in guys who had been there and won before—guys like Reggie McKenzie, Blair Bush, Charle Young, and Cullen Bryant.

A lot of them were past their prime, maybe even over the hill. But they were intelligent, high-character guys who knew how to play and were winners. They were the perfect complement to a team with a lot of first-round draft picks that just didn't know how to win.

We were certainly talented. We had first-round picks such as Kenny Easley and Jacob Green and the new guy, Curt Warner. We had a few leaders such as Dave Brown and Steve Largent. But the one thing that was missing was a belief that we were good enough.

So when these veteran guys came in and told us this was the most talented team they had been on, we began to think that maybe we were good. They were leaders, guys who could mentor and inspire the young players. We had a great coaching staff and great youth, and Chuck infused it with veteran leadership that had been sorely lacking.

In player meetings, Reggie ran the court. No one messed with him. At age 33, he was definitely past his prime, at the end of his career. But we believed him when he said we were going to win. All year, he demanded that we believe in ourselves. He had been to the playoffs a lot, and he said we didn't take a backseat in talent to anybody in the league.

Charle had won a Super Bowl with the San Francisco 49ers. He also was a preacher, and when he spoke, his words were piercing. They rang loud and clear. So when he said we were the most talented team he had been on, we believed him.

Largent said he never faced defensive backs in games who were as good as the ones he went against in practice every day—Dave Brown, Kenny Easley, John Harris, and the rest of us.

It was brilliant of Chuck to bring those guys in because they gave us confidence. We were a team people were not expecting a lot from. But Chuck expected it. Chuck knew what he had. He knew this team was on the rise and had talented pieces. And he knew we were just missing some leadership and needed some good coaching.

We had a pretty good preseason. We lost 10–7 to a very good Denver team in the preseason opener, and Chuck just pumped us up and told us, "This should make you believe that you can compete against anybody."

We should have won the regular-season opener in Kansas City, but we lost 17–13, and Chuck was disappointed because we hadn't played as well as we were capable of playing.

The confidence started to grow a bit the next week when we beat the Jets 17–10 in New York. They had some big-time players, such as Joe Klecko and Mark Gastineau, and we dominated them physically. That was the first time we thought maybe we could win.

We beat San Diego 34–31 at home and then lost 27–17 at the Kingdome to the Washington Redskins, who had won the Super Bowl the previous season and were a physical, nasty team.

We won in Cleveland and then lost in San Diego when Jim Zorn threw an interception that the Chargers returned for the go-ahead touchdown. We managed to beat the Raiders 38–36 at the Kingdome, and that made us 4–3.

But we still didn't know how to win consistently. We were giving up points and turning the ball over and didn't have any rhythm.

Then came a home game against the Pittsburgh Steelers, which was the turning point of our season. We fell behind 21–0 at halftime, and Chuck decided to do something. He said, "We're better than this. I'm going to make a change at quarterback. I'll give you an opportunity to play. But if you're not getting it done, I'm putting the next guy in because this is a playoff football team."

Dave Krieg replaced Zorn in the second half of the game against Pittsburgh, and Dave gave us a boost of adrenaline, a spark. And we all thought, "This guy is a big-play quarterback."

One of the reasons we were down 21–0 to Pittsburgh was that we were kind of in awe. They were the team of the 1970s and still had some of those stars—Franco Harris, John Stallworth, Jack Lambert, Mel Blount, Donnie Shell. They were legends. We wanted to go get their autographs, not beat them in a football game. Just like games we lost against Washington and Dallas, it was kind of surreal playing those Steelers.

Half the battle for Chuck was, "I gotta get these guys thinking they're not only NFL players but elite NFL players."

And when Krieg came into that Pittsburgh game, we learned we could play with anybody, and—even though we fell short, 27–21—we gained a bit of a swagger.

We won Dave's first two starts, beating the Raiders 34–21 in Los Angeles and Denver 27–19 in the Kingdome. We were 6–4 at that point, but then we lost shootouts in St. Louis (33–28) and Denver (33–27).

We were giving up so many points because we just didn't know how to play team defense yet. We used to run this triangle defense, where there was a lot of switching and passing receivers off in coverage. That doesn't come right away. It comes with experience and guys talking to each other. We were giving up points not because of a lack of talent but because of a lack of execution.

We gave up even more points the next week against Kansas City, but we beat the Chiefs 51–48 in what was then the highest-scoring game in NFL history. Curt Warner ran for a team-record 207 yards and three touchdowns, and Norm Johnson kicked a 42-yard field goal with two seconds left to send the game into overtime and then hit another one shortly thereafter to win.

At that point, we started to feel like a team of destiny. We didn't care how many points we were giving up. All we cared about was winning. The attitude was, "We won 51–48? Great. Good job, defense. Way to stop them on that last drive."

We got blown out by Dallas the next week, dropping us to 7–7 on our way to New York to play the Giants. We got some more help from the football gods in that one when the Giants had a go-ahead touchdown pass nullified by a penalty against a guy who had been holding Jacob Green all game. It was a no-brainer holding call. Jacob got a great jump, and the guy pulled him down. If we had lost that game, we would have missed the playoffs.

After the 51–48 overtime win and the big victory against the Giants, we were starting to feel like maybe we were a team of destiny. We went home to host New England in a winner-take-all game for the playoffs, and we thumped them. It was a butt-kicking on both sides of the football. We won 24–6, but it felt like 45–0. It was one of those games.

With that, we were in the playoffs for the first time in franchise history. There's nothing like the first time you have a chance at the playoffs. The crowd was jacked up. The town was shut down. All the talk was Seahawks. We had never experienced it before, even though Seattle was a football town.

We went into the playoffs on a roll and playing with great confidence, and we blew out the Broncos 31–7 in the first round. The Broncos had rookie quarterback John Elway, but they started Steve DeBerg in that game.

Our defense was coming together. We had given up 12, 6, and 7 points in the previous three games. We were getting the scheme. We weren't thinking as much as we had been early in the season. It took until the final few games to get it together, but we were feeling pretty good about ourselves at that point. We were young and felt no pressure.

When we went to Miami, we were huge underdogs. Quarterback Dan Marino had set records all year as a rookie, and here we were, a Northwest team flying all the way across country to play in Miami. No one expected us to win. But Chuck really sold us that we had a great game plan and were going to win this game. We believed it.

Part of our defensive plan was to take away their top receivers, who were big-play guys, and not let Marino beat us. Toward the end of the first half, they went into a two-minute offense and were driving on us. And they were doing it by dumping the ball to their running backs.

With 40 seconds left and third down, Easley told defensive coordinator Tom Catlin that we needed to go to the dime package to stop their backs from turning those short passes into big gains. Easley was really smart, and when he was into the game like that, there was no question in my mind we were going to win the game. It also showed what kind of a coach Catlin was that in a playoff game he listened to one of his players and made a quick personnel change. I happened to be the seventh defensive back in that package, and I did exactly what Kenny told me. We stopped them from scoring before halftime and extending their 13–7 lead.

We were up 17–13 in the fourth quarter with 4:34 left when Krieg and Largent had a miscommunication that gave the ball back to Miami. The Dolphins were blitzing, and Dave threw a slant route while Largent was running a fade, and the Dolphins intercepted. They drove down and scored a touchdown.

That really deflated us, and the doubts started creeping in a little bit. We were waiting for something to happen, and then Krieg and Largent did it. We were down 20–17 with under four minutes left, and Krieg and Largent connected on a 40-yard gain down to the Miami 2-yard line.

Steve could run a corner route better than anybody in the league. He was so good at getting separation from the cornerback. On that play, the Dolphins played single coverage with a safety on top, and singling the best receiver in the league was a bad call. Krieg and Largent had run that corner route a thousand times in practice. And they did it just like practice there. Krieg read Largent's move and threw a perfect pass for a huge gain. Then Curt Warner ran it off right tackle from the 2 for the touchdown that put us back in the lead, 24–20, with under two minutes left. We were going nuts on the sideline.

Normally you squib kick it in that situation. But we kicked away because Chuck and special-teams coach Rusty Tillman had such faith in our coverage teams. We had some good cover guys. And they came through. Sam Merriman recovered a fumble by Fulton Walker, and we kicked a field goal to take a 27–20 lead. They fumbled on the next kickoff, too, and we just ran out the clock on the biggest win in Seahawks history.

It was a great way to celebrate New Year's Eve. We had chartered a bigger plane than we normally did because we had a big entourage with us and didn't want to have to refuel on the way home. It was a party on the plane. We had cases and cases of champagne. It was a great experience, a great bonding time. We had a six-hour party.

When we landed at Sea-Tac Airport, they wanted to take us upstairs to the terminal because they said there were some fans waiting for us. The windows were all fogged up, so we couldn't see that there were actually thousands of people. There were 10,000 people there, and it took two hours for Norm Johnson and I to drive out of the terminal with our dates.

Norm and I went downtown to Pier 70 to celebrate that night. They had the red carpet out for us and some other players who were there. It was the presidential treatment, complete with a magnum of champagne. The place was packed, and everyone was celebrating. It was the greatest fan-related football experience of my life. We felt like kings that night.

Three days later, I was doing an autograph session at SouthCenter Mall with another backup player, and there were 2,000 people waiting for us to sign autographs. The line was wrapped around SouthCenter and back through the mall. We signed for hours, past the time of closing. That's how big the Seahawks were back then. We were not even starters, and we were treated like royalty.

We already had beaten the Raiders twice that season, so we were confident as we got ready to play them in the AFC Championship Game. We got even more excited during a players-only meeting leading up to the game when Charle Young brought out two boxes. He opened one and took out the NFC Championship ring he had won with the 49ers. He showed it to us and said, "Fellas, win this game, and we get this ring right here." Then he brought out his Super Bowl ring and said, "For a chance to win this ring." It probably was one of the best speeches ever. It was amazing to see the players' reaction when he brought those rings out. Most of us had never seen a Super Bowl ring before. Everyone just looked at each other wordlessly and knew then what we were playing for.

But when we got on the field with the Raiders, they were ready for us. They hated us because we were an upstart bunch that had swept them, and they didn't want to just beat us—they wanted to embarrass us. And they did. We lost 30–14, and it wasn't really that close. They led 27–0 late in the third quarter, and we scored only when Zorn replaced Krieg and threw two late touchdown passes, including one with under two minutes left. We could have played our best game of the year, and we still would have lost. The Raiders were that dominant and went on to beat the Redskins in the Super Bowl.

But we had turned into a contender. We were now a team that believed in itself. After that experience, we thought we would be the team to beat going into 1984.

In 1984 We Lost Warner but Not Our Drive

Most experts had us with Miami and the Raiders as the best teams in the AFC entering the 1984 season. There was a lot of talk about Warner possibly breaking O.J. Simpson's season rushing record (2,003 yards), our defense had a lot of talent, and we had a great coaching staff. The sky was the limit. We were no longer over-achievers. Our sights were legitimately set on the Super Bowl.

In one season, we had gone from being a young, inexperienced team to a veteran team that expected big things. We had great camaraderie, and our offense and defense both were talented and comfortable in their schemes.

We went 4–1 in the preseason, and we felt like we were better than anyone, that all we had to do was walk on the field and we would win. We were feeling kind of cocky going into the opener against Cleveland. We had a chip on our shoulder and wanted to kill teams, to blow them away. And we felt we could do it. We started off against Cleveland, and it was happening just like we thought it should—we were blowing them out. And then the worst thing that could happen happened. The Kingdome AstroTurf grabbed Warner. His foot got caught in the turf, and he blew out his ACL. It's still the worst injury to a team that the Seahawks have ever had as far as the on-field impact.

We blew out Cleveland 33–0 and became the first Seahawks team to win its opener. But the mood was pretty low because we had lost Curt.

Chuck Knox was a master motivator, though, and he said this team was not about one person. It's about a system and guys playing together. He didn't say it wasn't a big blow, but he asked, "Who's going to step up and fill the void? You all now have to raise your level of play."

Just as Chuck had done in 1983, bringing in veteran guys to build the morale of the team, he did it again in 1984 when Curt went down. We were all looking around, going, "Now what?" And he brought in Franco Harris, who had been let go by the Steelers before the season.

We all thought that was a good move, to bring in a veteran workhorse back with four Super Bowl rings. We all knew about the Immaculate Reception, and when Franco walked into the locker room, he became an immediate celebrity.

The first couple of games, Franco did pretty well, but you could see he didn't have it anymore. He's such a small part of the history of the Seahawks, but he was an important part of it at the time. He was the kind of guy who could fit in with everybody, and he really helped our team bond.

By bringing in Franco Harris, Chuck let us figure out who we were as a team without focusing too much on what we didn't have. Even though Franco was with us for only eight games, his presence comforted us and made us think we were going to be okay without Curt.

And we were. Even without our rushing star, we had a magical season. We started 4–2 and then won eight straight, which was a team record until the 2005 Seahawks won 11 straight on the way to the Super Bowl.

In 1984 we went from Ground Chuck with Curt Warner to not having Curt and Dave Krieg having to shoulder the offense. He had started only half the season the year before. And now everything was on Dave. We were no longer a strong running team. We became an efficient passing team.

We relied a lot on Steve Largent, but along the way we found a deep threat, too. Daryl Turner was a rookie receiver with long strides and long arms. Largent caught 12 touchdown passes that year, and Turner had 10. He scored once every 3.5 catches that year and still holds the team record for career yards per catch (18.5). He was perfect in that offense, which stressed ball control and mixed in deep passes. When we played in Denver late that season, we opened the game with an 80-yard touchdown pass from Krieg to Turner. I'd never seen anything like it. We beat Denver 27–24 that game, and we set the tone with that bomb to Turner.

Another reason we won in 1984 is that we had one of the best defenses in NFL history, a ballhawking unit like we'd never had. We had 38 interceptions, a team record that probably will never be broken. And we had 63 total turnovers, which is still the second most in NFL history (the 1961 San Diego Chargers had 66).

It was amazing. We all believed we were going to make plays. It wasn't about not making mistakes. Chuck, Tom Catlin, and Rusty Tillman said, "Don't be afraid to make a mistake. Be excited to make a play." They praised the big play so much that you wanted to be part of that. Instead of hoping the quarterback wouldn't throw it in your direction, you thought, "Throw it my way, please. I've got to get an interception."

The tone was set by Kenny Easley, Dave Brown, and John Harris, who were always stripping the ball in practice. We weren't interested in forcing three-and-outs. We wanted to go one and out.

We were all getting interceptions and other turnovers. Easley led the league with 10 interceptions and was named NFL Defensive Player of the Year. Brown had eight interceptions, and he and Easley returned two each for touchdowns. Jeff Bryant led the team with 14.5 sacks and also had an interception and two fumble recoveries. Jacob Green had 13 sacks and four fumble recoveries. Harris had six picks and a fumble pickup. Nose tackle Joe Nash had seven sacks and three fumble recoveries. We got standout performances from so many guys, and yet only three of them made the Pro Bowl—Easley, Brown, and Nash.

The defense clicked and came together as a playmaking team. It was about risk-reward. We knew how much risk it took to get that reward. And we were rewarded pretty handsomely.

If we had had Curt Warner that year, we would have gone to the Super Bowl and played the 49ers. Unfortunately, we started looking at the standings. We knew we needed Miami to lose. We knew we were going to play them; we were the two best teams. Every single week, Miami and we were looking at each other as we battled for home-field advantage in the playoffs.

We were 12–2 when we went to Kansas City, where the Chiefs were always a thorn in our side. We had everything to play for, we were the hottest team in the NFL, and we got crushed 34–7. All of the confidence we had built that year was lost in one game. That magic disappeared overnight.

We not only lost home-field advantage throughout the playoffs, we were suddenly playing to win the AFC West against Denver in the season finale. And the Broncos blew us out at home, 31–14, and won the West. We ended up a wild-card with a 12–4 record—that showed how tough the AFC was that year.

Entering the playoffs, we had lost confidence and had no identity. All of a sudden, our warts were exposed. We couldn't run it. We couldn't protect the quarterback. Our defense had lived off turnovers that year and now was giving up too many points.

Our first playoff game was a rematch of the previous season's AFC title game against the Raiders, except this time it was at the Kingdome. We were missing left tackle Ron Essink and had to start Sid Abramowitz, a guy some thought couldn't have played in the Pac-10 that year. Chuck didn't like the idea of Abramowitz facing Howie Long, so the game plan was to run the ball…then run the ball some more…and then run the ball even more. We ended up running it 49 times. We gained 202 yards and held the ball for about 10 minutes longer than the Raiders did, as we held on to win 13–7.

We threw just 10 times, and Long beat Abramowitz and hit Krieg on nine of the 10 passes. We were just counting the minutes down until the end of the game. We just thought, "Don't turn it over, run the clock out, hold the lead, and don't give up any big plays."

It was a big win because they were the defending Super Bowl champions, and we had lost to them the year before. Unfortunately, we had to fly to Miami again. And they were ready for us this time. It wasn't close. They beat us up pretty good that day, 31–10.

But with our success in 1983 and 1984, we had become one of the AFC's top teams, and we stayed that way for the rest of the decade.

Chuck Knox

I (Moyer) played for Chuck Knox for seven years and coached for him for two years. During our tenure together, we really didn't have a lot of deep conversations. Chuck was a man of few words, and he tended to surround himself with people he felt comfortable with.

Chuck and I had a different relationship than he had with the other coaches. It seemed like there was a generation gap, and at times I almost felt like he was uncomfortable around me. I would define the relationship as his being more of a father figure to me than a colleague. He spoke to me only a few times in nine years. But when he spoke, they were meaningful words.

I was a huge Chuck Knox fan because I grew up in Orange County, California, when he was coaching the Rams. I idolized the guy. So I was pretty excited when I was a rookie in 1983 and he came up to me while I was stretching during mini-camps and said, "Paul, welcome to Seattle. Glad to have ya."

In 1984 I was pretty sure I was going to make the team because I had had a pretty good rookie year. We were playing the

San Francisco 49ers in the preseason, and I didn't hit the tight end coming down the middle the way I normally would because it was the last preseason game. Chuck walked up to me during the next practice and said, "I'm a little concerned about your hitting." I said, "Coach, you don't have to worry about it." And he said, "I'm worried about it. You know why you're here, don't you? You're here to hit people. So fix it."

In 1988 we were playing the Houston Oilers in the Kingdome, and I intercepted a pass by Warren Moon in the end zone late in the game. We ended up winning, and Chuck came up to me afterward and said, "That was a good play. Couldn't have happened at a better time."

In 1989 I had a severe injury to my neck and was trying to figure out what to do. He walked up to me after he found out about the seriousness of my injury, and he told me, "You've had a good career. You need to retire. How would you like to start your coaching career here with us? I'd like you on the staff."

And that was about it. Those were my four major moments leading up to becoming an assistant.

It didn't change much when I became a coach.

When we were out socially as coaches and having a few cocktails, he would let his guard down a little bit and tell me, "You're a great coach. You're going to have a great career."

It's so funny because people ask, "Well, how come he hired you as a coach?" I said, "It was the ruptured testicle [in a 1986 game, recounted later in this book]." I just think he appreciated that kind of sacrifice. Anybody who would go to that length to play a game and do whatever it takes to win was his kind of guy.

In 1991 I (Wyman) had a bad preseason. I was not playing well the whole camp. The night before the opener against New Orleans, he called me over and said, "Dave, you know I love you, but if you keep playing the way you're playing, you're going to be standing on the sideline next to me." And then he walked away. And I said, "Oh, shit." I didn't work well under pressure, knowing I had to *not* screw up in order to keep my job.

Charles in Charge

I (Wyman) used to marvel at how the second Chuck walked into a room, it would get quiet. How do you establish that? You have to be someone people fear and respect.

He would tell a story about a player, and you would be convinced he was talking about you. He would never say the guy's name. But he would say something like, "Some scared cat didn't come up and make that tackle." And, every time, about 10 guys in the room would think, "Ah, shit, he's talking about me."

When he was across the field, he was like the Mona Lisa or those holograms at the Haunted Mansion in Disneyland—wherever you were standing, it looked like he was looking right at you.

We'd be stretching with 50 guys spread across the field, Chuck would be standing there with his cap pulled down over his eyes, and you still would swear he was looking right at you.

His assistant coaches weren't immune, either.

Chuck would never call out the assistant he was talking to, but he would just say things like, "I don't understand the damn defensive linemen on our team. What the hell are we coaching these guys?"

One time, he was grousing about the D-line again, and line coach George Dyer just stood up and winged his clipboard right over Chuck's head and walked out. Chuck just started laughing his ass off and said, "What got into him? What the hell was that all about?"

We had pretty good special teams in the 1980s under Rusty Tillman, and Chuck would motivate Rusty by saying things like, "I'm watching film, and Denver's special teams…have you seen them cover? Now that's a coverage unit."

Rusty would get ticked off and challenge Chuck right back. And Chuck liked that.

Chuck also liked to make sure we were doing our jobs. We could not leave evening meetings until Chuck left the building. Everyone would be done, and we'd be wondering, "Has Chuck had his last scotch? Is he gone? Paul, go out and check to see if his car's gone."

Why was Chuck such a great coach? Was it Xs and Os? Partly. Chuck really knew personnel very well. Ground Chuck threw the ball a whole lot for a guy who wanted to run it.

He would come into our defensive meetings, and he'd subtly point out things we should do: "Hey, now, we don't want Terry Taylor on an island against Art Monk. We're going to have a safety over there, right?" And we'd say, "Absolutely, Coach." Then he would leave, and we'd say to each other, "Okay, let's make sure we shift our safeties over a little bit."

He would say, "I want playmakers. I never want to take that away from you. But if you don't make the play or do the assignment correctly, you're wrong."

He had a message he would send in the form of a pop-quiz question: "There are two guys running deep down the field. You're the only defender. Which one do you cover?" Answer: "The one they throw the ball to." His point was: "Make the right decision and just make the play."

This extended beyond football.

Chuck and I (Moyer) were golfing down in Palm Springs, paired up against some other guys. I missed a six-foot putt, and we lost, and he blamed it on me. I shot about a 75, and he shot a 90. But I missed a six-foot putt, and it was my fault. That was his competitiveness.

"That About Covers It"

Chuck was very detailed and a master motivator. Everything he did was thought out and done for a reason. He would spend hours preparing for our morning meetings, and the Saturday evening speech was no different. He knew how fine a line there was between winning and losing, so he would exploit any edge he could find. If he could get his team to hate the other team or play with an attitude, then, by God, he was going to find a way of motivating his players.

Chuck had some legendary pregame speeches. The unfortunate thing was they always came on Saturday nights in the hotel instead of right before kickoff in the locker room. They were always good talks that would get you plenty fired up. The problem was you were pumped full of adrenaline and had to go up to your room and try to get to sleep. It's hard enough to go to sleep the night before a game without that. I (Wyman) remember lying wide-eyed in my hotel room before many a Seahawks game.

Chuck was known to like his scotch and would typically have a couple of glasses before his Saturday evening speeches. The scotches certainly added to the fire and passion of his talks. These were never G-rated; and, one time in particular, the speech was R-rated.

In 1988 we were at home against the Buffalo Bills, who led the league in quarterback sacks that year. The Bills didn't just sack the quarterback; they stood over him and did a celebration dance. I'm sure it was funny to them and their fans, but it was infuriating to opposing players and coaches.

Chuck was particularly outraged by this, so in lieu of his usual "Storm the Bastille" speech, he had Thom Fermstad, our video director, put together a highlight reel of the Bills' sack dances. As the film played, Chuck ranted about the amount of disrespect displayed. The longer the film played, the more obscene Chuck's language got. He was hot.

The film ended, the lights were turned on, and Chuck got up and swaggered past me (Wyman) and out of the room. I picked up a faint whiff of what had undoubtedly fueled his fire as he walked past me. The room was left dead quiet, and no one moved except for Steve Largent, who was seated in the first row, right next to where Chuck had been sitting. As the door closed behind Chuck and the lights came on, Steve turned around in his chair, looked at the entire room of players, and just shook his head in a very disapproving manner.

Usually at this point, Rusty Tillman would go through a meeting and put on film. Instead, Rusty stood up and said, "Well, I think that about covers it," and dismissed the meeting.

I always enjoyed the broad spectrum of personalities in the NFL. And here was a great contrast. On one end was a Boy Scout who disapproved of foul language, and on the other end was an assistant coach who thought what he had just heard was spot on.

We ended up losing to the Bills 13–3. But it certainly wasn't for lack of inspiration.

In Denver one year, I (Wyman) found myself sitting in the front row during another one of Chuck's impassioned speeches. He had just come out of a press conference in which a reporter had asked him a few skeptical questions. One of the questions was in reference to the fact that we had not had very much success playing in Denver. The reporter had asked him, "Isn't this the same old crew [team] that you've brought here the last few years?"

As Chuck related this story to us in the meeting, I happened to look up just as he told us his response to the question. "I got your same old crew right here!" he said, grabbing his crotch.

I appreciated his sticking up for us, but I could have done without the visual. As I winced and turned away, the entire room erupted in laughter.

Chuck defended us on the field, too. He was notorious for berating the referees on the sideline. He felt his main job was to manage the clock and work the refs in our favor, and he was pretty good at it.

Chuck would study the numbers of each ref and know everything he could about them so during the game he would always know each one by his first name and even mother's name if he could. And he would rip them if he felt they made a bad call or weren't calling the game fairly.

Dressed to Impress

Chuck used to love going down to Los Angeles because all of the movie stars would come out. We'd be down in Century City, and that was his time to shine. They loved Chuck, who had coached the Los Angeles Rams before he came to Seattle.

When he was down in L.A., that was his scene. He was very comfortable hobnobbing with the celebrities because he fit right in. He was a Sinatra type of guy the way he walked around and carried himself.

He never talked about his money, but image was important. He'd wear his gold Rolex and gold chain, he had that big diamond ring that said "CK" on it, and he always had his nails manicured. He used to wear the Bill Cosby sweaters and all of the stylish stuff. He dressed to impress and command respect.

It was all about image. Chuck was very orchestrated in everything he did. Impressions were important.

He used to get on me (Wyman) about the way I dressed (sweatshirts and jeans): "All the money you make, you oughta be out buying some nicer clothes." I remember thinking, "Chuck, I make a quarter of what you make."

When I (Moyer) was coaching, Chuck used to say that it was important the head coach make as much as the highest-paid player because it reflected the hierarchy. You've got to have that respect. So he was always up there as high as our top-paid players. When he left, he was probably making a million dollars a year, which was near the top of the league.

He also used to say, "When you go out at night, leave a good tip. Otherwise, people around town are going to say, 'That guy is a cheap prick.'" And he would emphasize the Ps. Chea*p p*rick.

He was always talking about tipping people well and taking care of people. "Don't give the team or the players a bad name."

One of his favorite sayings when we had time off was, "Don't throw the ball so far over the fence that you can't go get it."

His point was that we should strive to be responsible, reputable citizens and role models. Reputation and perception were important to him, and he tried to get that message across all of the time.

He had many more pet phrases that we all refer to as Knoxisms:

- Bring your hard hat and lunch bucket.
- Play the hand you're dealt.
- When a man hits the ground, a man gets up.
- Don't tell me how rough the water is. Just bring the boat in.
- Don't piss in my face and tell me it's raining.
- The six Ps: Proper preparation prevents piss poor performance.

- Practice does not make perfect; perfect practice makes perfect.
- Complain about nothin'. Do somethin'!
- Five plays decide the game. Who's going to get those five plays?
- Football players make football plays.

When he would say those, he would always look at Jeff Bryant, one of his favorite players, and say, "Isn't that right, Boogie?"

After nine years, some guys would say, "Oh, that's corny." But I (Moyer) still got fired up all the time.

After big wins, Chuck liked to take care of us. More than once, he pulled out his wallet or credit card and bought up all the beer in the place so we could celebrate. In 1990 we beat Kansas City on the last play—one of the best wins in franchise history. On the way to the plane, a few of us filed into a little bar in the airport. Chuck came walking into the bar looking very serious and stern. The place hushed, much like any time he walked into a meeting room. All of a sudden, he reached into his back pocket, pulled out his credit card, and put it on the bar. And everyone breathed a sigh of relief. Soon the place was full of players and coaches, and we emptied the bar out.

In 1986 we rallied to beat New England in dramatic fashion. It was a long bus ride back to the airport, and Chuck had the bus pull over at a little convenience store in the middle of nowhere. He handed his credit card to some players and sent them into the store to buy beer for everyone. They just about emptied the place out then, too.

The same thing happened one time in Los Angeles. I (Wyman) can still see nose tackle Roy Hart carrying eight cases of beer back to the bus. The cases were stacked up to his nose as he waddled out with all of this beer Chuck had bought for us.

Chuck didn't show much emotion and was hard to get to know, and he wouldn't tolerate mistakes and people who didn't do their jobs. But he also wasn't afraid to show his appreciation when they did. He was a man of few words, but one way or another Chuck always got his message across.

Curt Warner was perhaps Seattle's brightest football star during his prime in the 1980s.

Curt Warner

When Chuck Knox was hired by the Seahawks in 1983, he came from Buffalo, where his teams had run the ball well, and he was determined the Seahawks were going to get a great running back. Ground Chuck was old-school football and believed the way to a championship was a dominant defense and a great running game. Chuck felt so strongly about getting a great running back that the

Seahawks traded their first three picks, including the ninth overall, to Houston to move up to the number-three spot in the 1983 draft.

The two best running backs in the draft that year were Eric Dickerson and Curt Warner, both considered franchise players. John Elway was the top pick, the Los Angeles Rams selected Dickerson second, and the Seahawks got Warner to start what was perhaps the best draft in the history of the NFL.

Curt was a superstar immediately and a guy who was considered the savior, the one who could carry us to the playoffs. The Seahawks had never had a running back who was about to make the impact that Curt Warner would.

A Superstar His Entire Life

Curt came from the small town of Wyoming, West Virginia, where he was raised by his grandparents in a very small two-bedroom home on the river.

He went to a really small school, and a lot of college coaches never had a chance to watch him play football because he played out in the middle of nowhere. Penn State's Joe Paterno was one of those coaches who never got to see Curt play football, but Paterno had heard legendary stories about this young man from Wyoming, West Virginia, and decided he needed to see him for himself. It just so happened that Curt had a high school basketball game the evening Joe was coming to visit him. After watching Curt play, Joe offered him a scholarship based purely on his athleticism.

The West Virginia Mountaineers were not happy Curt was going to become a Penn State Nittany Lion. They felt Curt was a traitor for leaving his home state. But it wasn't long before 80,000 fans at State College, Pennsylvania, were chanting, "War-ner, War-ner, War-ner!"

In 1982 Curt and Todd Blackledge led Penn State to a national title, beating Herschel Walker and the undefeated Georgia Bulldogs 27–23 in the Sugar Bowl.

And then the Seahawks made their big move to bring Curt to Seattle. He had been a superstar his whole life. So when he came to Seattle, nothing changed.

Yes, we had Kenny Easley and Steve Largent, but Curt became the face of the team. Everyone wanted his attention. He was the one getting endorsement deals, ESPN interviews, and star treatment wherever we went. He came from a national championship team, had a big-time agent in Marvin Demoff, and signed a big contract. He made something like $800,000 his first year, which was big money back then. He had it all.

Even though we were from opposite worlds—a white guy from the big city out west and a black guy from a small town back east—Curt and I ended up becoming friends. We were both rookies in 1983, and we ended up as roommates because my first roommate snored so loudly I couldn't sleep and had to find a new roomie.

Curt and I didn't like each other at first. I thought he was spoiled and privileged and pampered, and he thought I was cocky. But it wasn't long before we became best friends. Curt had been raised well by his grandparents. He was genuinely a good person, a strong Christian guy, didn't get in trouble, and wanted to do the right thing.

He loved going to my house in California because my mother took care of us, and he could just relax there and get away from the pressures of NFL stardom.

That Glazed Look

Our rookie year, those pressures included plenty of abuse from the veteran players.

Curt hated being the spokesperson for the rookies. He had to stand up every day in training camp and sing. He was actually a pretty good singer, but he had learned only about five songs coming into camp, and the veterans soon got tired of hearing the same songs over and over again. But Curt never wavered, and he did what he was told to do.

Curt also hated to give the Doughnut Report on Fridays during the season. We would have a players meeting every Friday afternoon, and Curt had to give the report of what type of doughnuts the rookies brought in that morning: "Paul Moyer brought 12 glazed, 12 maples, 12 sprinkles, 12 chocolates," etc.

Reggie McKenzie didn't like glazed doughnuts, and he told the rookies not to buy the glazed kind anymore. One Friday, when it was Curt's turn to buy the doughnuts, he decided to spite Reggie by buying only glazed doughnuts. When it was time for the Doughnut Report, Curt stood military-style and reported, "Curt Warner brought 60 glazed doughnuts."

Reggie was hot, but Curt was very defiant, telling Reggie, "If you want maples, get them yourself!"

Curt thought that was the funniest thing in the world and was very proud that he had stood up to them. He hated being a rookie.

He also came to dislike all of the media attention that was showered on him. During the season, he had a lot of demands on his time, particularly with interviews. It got to the point that he would say, "I'm not doing it." He was tired from practice, had to spend time in the training room when he was banged up, and then the PR guys wanted him to do more interviews. He just wanted a break.

Every once in a while, the team PR guys would ask me to talk to him because I was his closest friend on the team. They would say, "Just this once. It's Al Michaels." So I would pass on the message: "Just this one, C-Dub." And he would protest, "No, I'm not doing it this time." But he would almost always give in and do it. He would complain the whole time, but he would do it.

Curt Was a Shy Superstar

Believe it or not, Curt was actually kind of shy. Yeah, he was a number-one draft pick, the star of the team, the spokesperson at times, very articulate, and people liked him because he was a great guy. But when he got around a large group of people, he was kind of a fish out of water. It was funny to watch because he was so successful and such a star, but being from a small town and being very protected at Penn State, he never had to deal with a large group of people before he got to the NFL.

He was confident in himself, but he wasn't naturally outgoing. When someone like Whitney Houston would come to town, he was always invited backstage. He would accept the invitations, but he wasn't always comfortable in those situations. He would want me to go with him, but they would always stop me at the back door, and he'd be on his own. And I would say, "Well, I want to meet Whitney. I'll strike up a conversation with her, and he won't."

Curt liked to go to Los Angeles with me and hang out. He didn't mind being well known because it got us into places a lot of people couldn't get into. But down in L.A., people didn't recognize him as much, and he could relax and be himself. When someone did recognize him, he was always gracious enough to sign an autograph.

Early in his career, Curt thought he might like to be an actor. He took acting classes in his first couple of years and did local theater. He worked hard at it and was willing to start from the bottom and humble himself to become the best. He had the fame to maybe catapult it, but in the end he didn't really want it that much. That wasn't the type of life he wanted to live. He didn't want that kind of celebrity.

He would put his amateur thespian skills to work around friends, though. Curt could have kind of a high-pitched voice, and he loved to mimic Wayne Cody, who was one of the big TV and radio personalities in Seattle sports back then. When my daughter was born, Curt videotaped it, and all I could here in the background was one of Wayne's signature phrases:

"Hello, everybody. Wayne Cody here. Hello, everybody. Wayne Cody here." Over and over again. "Hello, everybody. Wayne Cody here. Hello, everybody. Wayne Cody here." He beat it to death.

Curt was like a little kid at times. Once he found something that was funny, he would run with it.

Of course, he ran with the ball a whole lot better than he ever did with the jokes.

The Rise, Fall, and Triumphant Return of Curt Warner

The second we saw Curt hit the field, it was magical. On his very first run in 1983, he broke down the sideline 60 yards against Kansas City, and we all said, "This is a Hall of Fame running back." Even though he fumbled the ball on that carry (I remind him of that all the time) and we ended up losing 17–13, that game showed just how special he was.

He would make people miss, he would jump over piles, and he would even try to run guys over. He had such great stop-start ability. He had it all as a running back. He was one of the few people in the league who could run past you, make you miss, run through you, and—if he had to—jump over you.

He was definitely the franchise. With some help from new linemen Blair Bush and McKenzie in 1983, Curt ran for a team-record 1,449 yards, scored 13 touchdowns, and averaged 4.3 yards per carry. He was everything Chuck Knox had hoped for when we drafted him with the third pick and was an integral reason for us making the playoffs in 1983.

Curt was an instinctive runner, unlike any ever seen in Seattle. You just needed to tell him where the play was designed to go, then shut up and let him go. And where the play goes, no one knows. As a coach, the best thing you could do with Curt was build his confidence. You can't coach what Curt had. You can't coach instincts, vision, cutting ability.

The coaches would get mad and frustrated at times because Curt freelanced. They wanted him to hit a hole a certain way, but Curt was a run-to-daylight back, and he wouldn't always stay with the original hole like they wanted. Chick Harris, our running backs coach, would try to coach him to stay with the play. But Curt would get frustrated and say, "It's not there. They don't see what I see."

Coaching Curt was different than coaching the other running backs. You really had to let Curt do his thing. Because he showed in his rookie year just what he could do.

Going into 1984, Reggie had T-shirts made that simply had the number "2,004," which was the number of yards Warner would need to set the NFL rushing record. O.J. Simpson had run for 2,003 yards with Buffalo in 1973, and Reggie had been part of the Electric Company line that blocked for O.J. that year. Reggie and the rest of the O-line thought Curt could break O.J.'s record in 1984. They worked hard as a unit going into the '84 season, and no one doubted they would make a run at the record.

But in the first game against Cleveland, Curt went down with a torn knee ligament. You knew it was bad by the way he went to the ground. It was surreal because it was one of the few times I ever remember the Kingdome being so quiet. You could have heard a pin drop because everyone knew the seriousness of what had just happened.

The injury was tough. It was emotional. And it was painful for Curt.

But he was determined to come back better than ever, and he worked his butt off to get back for the 1985 season. In those days, coming back from an ACL injury was a 50-50 proposition. Not everyone made it back. It wasn't the sure thing that it typically is today.

Our running game suffered without Curt. After rushing for 2,119 yards in 1983 and averaging 3.9 per carry, we dropped off to 1,645 and 3.3 in 1984. Our top three rushers were David Hughes, Dan Doornink, and Eric Lane, and none of them went over 400 yards in 1984. We went 12–4 and made the playoffs again on the arm of Dave Krieg and the stellar play of our defense.

In 1985, with Warner back, we were picked as a Super Bowl favorite based on our success the previous year without him. Warner had a pretty good year in 1985, but his knee was sore a lot. After every practice and game, he was icing and stretching it. It really took until 1986 for him to come fully back—physically and mentally. He had his best season that year—breaking his own team record with 1,486 yards, rushing for 13 touchdowns, and averaging 4.6 per carry.

Curt was back. After a very difficult, emotional time in 1984, he was back to the jovial superstar we all knew and loved.

A Star Drives Off into the Sunset

Curt always enjoyed special star treatment, and it only got worse once he came back. Fans and teammates would often hold their collective breaths as Curt slowly picked himself up after plays. He had always been a slow riser—he said it was to conserve energy—but people always watched him anxiously after his injury.

Curt would play hard and get beat up in games—he never shied away from a hit—but he took advantage of his star status during the week. In practice, he didn't always have to do what everybody else had to do. It was a well-deserved perk.

While many treated him like a superstar, I felt it was my job as his friend to keep his head on his shoulders and his feet on the ground. Or, in one case, off the ground.

In 1989 he was running down on a kickoff as part of the scout team, and he wasn't running very hard. And I thought, "Here's the leader of our team, and he's dogging it." So I cold-cocked him—cheap-shotted him—just to teach him a lesson.

He was hot. And when he got upset, he would get a high-pitched voice. So he jumped up and said, "Hey, what was that all about!?" He didn't know whether to hit me or to laugh.

The 1986 season was unfortunately the pinnacle of Curt's career. He was hurt a lot in 1987 and missed the playoff game against Houston with an ankle injury. And in 1988 John L. Williams became more of a factor; he had a better average and was big in the passing game. Curt averaged just 3.9 yards per run, but he scored 10 touchdowns and was still a big part of the team as we won the division title for the first time.

The 1989 season was Curt's last as a Seahawk. You could see that the wear and tear from the Kingdome AstroTurf and the knee injury from 1984 had taken a big toll on him. He just wasn't as productive as he had been. We had turned from a running team to passing team. We went from Ground Chuck to Air Chuck, and Curt became less and less of a factor in the offense. He was beat up and carried only 194 times in 1989. His contract was up, and management thought his best years were behind him, so the team let him go.

He was bitter about that and hurt by it. He thought he could still play, and it was humbling for him that the Seahawks didn't want him anymore.

He ended up signing with the Rams and went to Los Angeles feeling excited about rejuvenating his career. But he had lost a step, due to the injury and to AstroTurf. It was hard to see him in another uniform. It didn't look right. And it didn't last long. He retired after the 1990 season.

He was prepared for the inevitable retirement. In the off-season, he had always worked on something. Early in his career, it was acting. Later, he found a passion for the car industry. He worked his tail off at dealerships doing every job they had so he could learn everything about the business. He wanted a career path when he was done with football. He wanted to be respected as a good businessman. And by the time he retired, he was ready to run his own business, so he bought a dealership. Curt didn't want to be a silent partner with his name attached to it; he wanted to run it. And he has been involved with Curt Warner Chevrolet ever since.

Curt Warner was a superstar from the day he arrived in Seattle. He was drafted to carry the Seahawks to the playoffs, and he did it. He had a stellar rookie season, rebounded from a horrible knee injury, and set every record in team history by the time his seven-year career was over.

Curt made the same kind of impact as teammates such as Steve Largent, Kenny Easley, and Dave Krieg. If not for the knee injury and the beating he took on AstroTurf, Curt most likely would have been a Hall of Famer. As it was, few players made the impact on the Seahawks that Curt Warner did.

chapter 3
1987

Kenny Easley wrestles down Mark Duper of the Dolphins during a 1984 playoff game in Miami.

The Strike

We had won our last five games in 1986 and barely missed the playoffs despite a 10-6 record. So we addressed one of our weakest positions by drafting linebackers Dave Wyman, Tony Woods, and Brian Bosworth, and we said, "This is it. These are the missing ingredients to take us to the next level."

The 1987 season was supposed to be our year—we were favorites to win the AFC and go to the Super Bowl—but instead it turned into one of the most disappointing seasons ever.

It started early as we got blown out in Denver, 40-17. Bosworth had almost single-handedly turned the game into a rivalry between himself and John Elway because of the whole "Boz versus Mr. Ed" thing. It was a circus.

We demolished Kansas City 43-14 at the Kingdome in week two, and then we went on strike, and things were never the same.

Wyman and Moyer viewed the strike differently. While they both did not like the way NFLPA president Gene Upshaw handled it, they saw it from different angles. Moyer was a veteran who had worked his way from undrafted free agent to key role player and never was paid that highly, while Wyman was a rookie who had never been part of a union.

Paul Moyer:

I remember going down to Century City, California, before the 1987 season started for an NFL union meeting. There were about 600 players there, and the room was divided on the course of action we should take against the owners. Todd Christensen was particularly adamant that the union should hire Donald Fehr to represent us. Baseball seemed to have its act together, and it made sense to have someone with experience take the lead. But Gene Upshaw was convinced he and his staff knew the issues best, and this was the direction the NFL union was heading. The strange thing was most of the players didn't trust Gene Upshaw, but no one knew how to get rid of him. So when the strike finally took place, the players were clearly not united.

Dave Wyman:

The strike was ridiculous to me, but I was just a rookie so I went along with the whole thing. My agent, Marvin Demoff, told me from the outset, "Look, these are going to be your teammates for a long time. Whatever they decide, stick with your team." So I did.

Another thing he told me was that there was no reason to strike. He explained that it was clearly an antitrust lawsuit just waiting to happen, and that what we needed to do was to get the NFL in court after the season ended. He even mentioned Judge David Doty in the U.S. district court in Minnesota by name. He called the whole thing from the very beginning.

I relayed all of this to Blair Bush, who I viewed as the most intelligent and even-keeled guy on the team. That night at a meeting at Mike Tice's Fill Yer Belly Deli, Blair caught me a little off guard. Instead of just telling everyone what I said, he introduced me and had me deliver Marvin's message. I put it like this: "I know I'm just a rookie and don't know what's going on, but my agent is pretty smart—he specializes in labor law—and here's what he thinks."

The second I finished, union rep Kenny Easley totally discounted everything I said. In other words, it was treated the same way I remember everything else being treated by the union. There was never any room for alternative thinking.

I don't blame Kenny for that, and I never lost one bit of respect for him as a player, but he embodied what I came to know over the years as a typical union rep. He was toeing the NFLPA line, and dissension was not tolerated. In my view, the NFLPA has always operated like this: Gene Upshaw meets with all of the team reps, tells them what to say, and then sends them out to brainwash the rest of the team. It was like that on every team I was ever on. And the second anyone questioned the message, the union would typically respond angrily and in a very close-minded fashion.

At a union meeting in Denver one year, Upshaw was there in person, and when Hugh Millen questioned Gene on a few things (like his salary), Gene started cursing and yelling, and the meeting was over. It reminded me of those movies where the union boss and his henchmen show up with baseball bats and torches and tell you what to think while they pound the bats into their hands.

Everything else about the strike was handled poorly, too. At most of the meetings, alcohol was served, and that tended to throw fuel on people's emotional fires. There were also a couple of meetings that a few wives showed up to. Even though their views may have been valid, it did not sit well with most of the team. And then, the image of millionaires showing up in their Mercedes-Benzes to walk the picket line was just embarrassing. We were putting ourselves out there like we were steel workers struggling to feed our families. Who in the world would feel sorry for us? It was a public-relations nightmare. A good leader would have steered us away from that.

Moyer:

When Steve Largent stood before the team and said he was going to cross the picket line because, he said, "I feel like I need to honor my contract and I owe it to my family," that didn't make a lot of sense to me because Steve was one of the highest-paid players on the team. "You're set for life," I thought. I understood he believed he had a contract to honor, but his contract with his teammates should have been stronger. I just felt that even though we didn't all agree with the way the union handled the situation, it was still all for one and one for all. Maybe I was naïve, but that's how I felt. I certainly wasn't pro union. I was a right-wing conservative growing up, but I believed loyalty to my fellow players was the strongest accountability I could have. I was very upset about his decision, and so were a lot of the players. We had a hard time with one of our main leaders walking away from us.

Kenny had a strong opinion about it, too: "We're either all in it or we're not in it," he said. And he really struggled with the fact that we were a weak union, that we were wavering and that guys like Joe Montana and Steve Largent were getting ready to cross the line. Most of the players who crossed the line were the ones who had the highest contracts, and Kenny had a hard time with that.

But I remember Kenny saying, "Look, we're going to have a difference of opinion. Let Steve be heard."

I respect Steve and Jeff Kemp for standing before the team. It had to be hard. I think most of the guys just felt, "Wow. We're all in the same boat here. Your reasons are no better than ours. You're definitely dividing the team." But they were men, and I respected them for that. But I don't know if that sense of abandonment ever went away for some guys.

None of us believed we should have struck on the third week. We already had done that in 1982. We thought we should have waited until the last game before the playoffs. At that point, we would have made all of our money, and it would have hurt the owners more because they get a lot of their revenue from the playoffs. But Gene Upshaw said, "No, no. It worked before. It will work again."

What was ironic in the end was that the players who crossed were the ones who benefited the most. Steve Largent signed the first million-dollar contract in Seahawks history. Norm Johnson became a free agent and kicked until 2000. Fredd Young was traded and received a five-year contract worth $4.5 million.

Guys like Joe Montana went on to receive lucrative contracts because of free agency. And the master of it all, Gene Upshaw, has a contract that pays him more than $7 million a year today. The players who ended up striking for the *league* ended up with nothing. Benefits never changed, and we lost out on three games. As a league, it was ridiculous to go on strike; we would have received what we wanted in court. And that's what later happened.

That's why Gene Upshaw is one of the most hated men in the NFL. There aren't many guys who have played in the NFL who like or respect him. He stood before a group of people and said, "This is not about money; it's not about free agency. This is about better benefits. This is about a better pension and retirement." And he was just flat lying.

Wyman:

I'll guarantee you that if Gene Upshaw were sitting here, he would tell me that I benefited from that strike. I signed a free-agent contract in Denver and got three times the money I could have gotten in Seattle. But the point is that we would have won those things without the strike. It wasn't because of anything he did. It was there to be had by anybody with an ounce of negotiation skills.

There's an old saying in business: "You don't get what you deserve; you get what you negotiate." But we were trying to play on people's sympathies rather than going to court and legally negotiating what was there to be had.

Moyer:

The sad thing that came out of it all was that the Nordstroms put the team up for sale. They were a company that didn't have union employees, and there was a definite conflict of interest with management and the union Seahawks. I really believe we embarrassed John Nordstrom.

One story that stands out was the time when the replacement players were being bused back to their hotels from the team facility. A bunch of players, most notably Greg Gaines, stood in front of the bus waving wooden bats. You could tell the replacement players were scared for their lives. It wasn't our finest hour as players. The Nordstroms weren't very happy, and neither was Chuck Knox. And that really was the beginning of the end.

Once Steve, Jeff, Norm, and Fredd crossed the line, I just thought, "Wow. How do we get this team back together?"

Wyman:

Of all the guys who crossed, I think Jeff Kemp got it the worst. Largent was a legend and pretty much beyond reproach. Norm was a kicker—no one cared what he did. Everybody knew Fredd was all about the money, and he was not known as a very good teammate to anyone.

But Jeff was new to the team and, in his words, "a bit of a goody two shoes." Before the strike, he actually wrote a statement of purpose in which he defined his principles.

He said, "The owners are not my opponents. Without them, I have no job. They can get another me, but I can't get another them. I signed a contract, and I didn't feel right about violating it."

Later, Jeff told me, "Unfortunately, it cost me the respect of a lot of my teammates."

Except for me. Who writes a statement of purpose? I respected him more than ever for that.

Moyer:

Once we came back, Chuck said basically, "You ought to thank the replacement players."

They kept receiver Jimmy Teal, which we thought they did just to make a point. We all talked about how we were going to rip his head off. And Chuck said, "You're not going to do anything to him. You guys should be thanking them. They had a better record than you guys did before the strike. And we have a chance to make the playoffs because of these guys."

I think he lost a little respect from the players because of that comment. But the coaches were great to us during the strike. They stayed out of it and knew they were caught in the middle. We were practicing every day on our own. As a group, we were ready to come back. Dave Krieg and Kenny Easley ran our player-organized practices. The coaches weren't supposed to have contact with us during the strike, but they were secretly passing practice and game plans to us so we would be ready to go when the strike finally ended.

When we finally came back, it just didn't feel the same as it had when we left after the Kansas City game. It felt like the organization talked down to us, like the owners and coaches didn't respect us. It was embarrassing because we came back with our tails between our legs. We looked stupid during the strike, and they had a tendency to remind us of our failures. I'm sure that was more perception than reality and a product of our sensitive egos being hurt. What I do know for a fact is this: the organization was never the same again.

That strike was emotionally draining, and it broke the franchise apart—ownership, coaches, players, everything.

We tried to come together the best we could as a team. We kicked the crap out of the Raiders, 35–13, in L.A. in our first game back. And we made the playoffs that year. But we lost to Houston in overtime in a game decided by an official's controversial call.

It just wasn't that Northwest, Nordstrom, fun-loving team anymore. The Nordstroms sold the team because of that strike. And then the Behrings came along in 1988.

We ended up winning the AFC West and going to the playoffs in 1988. But the franchise that had turned into a respected contender under the Nordstroms crumbled to pieces after 1988 and remained a mess for a decade under the Behrings' ownership. Not until Paul Allen, Mike Holmgren, and Tod Leiweke arrived did it feel like this was a franchise we could be proud of again.

Kenny Easley

(by Paul Moyer)

Kenny Easley was the finest athlete I've ever been around. He was a scratch golfer, he was a great Ping-Pong player, he could bowl, he could play tennis. He was drafted by the NBA. He returned punts for us and even lined up at cornerback at times. He was the most feared hitter in the NFL.

Ronnie Lott will tell you he was not the player Kenny Easley was. It blows me away that Kenny's not in the Hall of Fame. I understand the longevity issue, but Gale Sayers got there, and he had an injury that took him out after seven seasons—the same length as Kenny's career.

Kenny Easley was NFL Defensive Player of the Year in 1984. As a safety. That was almost unheard of. Since the award was created in 1971, only three safeties have won it. Easley was the second. That's how rare it is for a safety to dominate a season like Easley did in 1984, when he tied a team record with 10 interceptions.

One of the best one-on-one matchups in the NFL back then was Kenny Easley against Raiders tight end Todd Christensen.

Kellen Winslow was a great route runner, and Ozzie Newsome was very good, but the best all-around tight end was Todd Christensen because he could block, he was nasty, he had great hands, and he simply was a gamer.

Todd was the guy you didn't want to face. Everyone double-teamed him, but Kenny Easley would say, "No, he's mine."

In a 3-4 defense like we ran, a linebacker usually was lined up over the tight end. But Kenny would walk up and kick the linebacker out of coverage so that he could cover Todd by himself. And Kenny and Todd would go at it all day. It was like a heavyweight fight, with Kenny always throwing the first punch. Todd was their best player at the time, and Kenny completely neutralized him. That's how good Kenny was.

Christensen thought Easley was even more impressive than San Francisco's Ronnie Lott, who was voted into the Hall of Fame in 2000. Christensen once said, "It goes without saying what Ronnie did in his career. But in all candor—and this is no knock on Ronnie—Kenny Easley was a better football player."

Kenny made the plea many times to move to free safety because teams would take him out of the game by putting a running back or tight end in motion, and, as the strong safety, Kenny would have to follow him even though he was just a decoy to lead Kenny away from the play. Kenny was adamant that he should have been the free safety, and he probably was right. He wanted to be involved in the game and make an impact, and he didn't feel he could do that consistently at strong safety.

In 1984 we shut out the San Diego Chargers on *Monday Night Football*. This was Dan Fouts, Kellen Winslow, Charlie Joiner, and that high-powered offense, and we were playing them in San Diego. There was a goal-line stand at one point, and Kenny was really into it, telling us they weren't going to get in. We were ahead 24–0, but he was so pumped to shut them out on national TV. Kenny already had two interceptions in that game, and it was arguably the greatest game I've ever seen played by one guy.

On their last drive, he cut across the field and made an incredible interception, sealing the shutout. It just showed his competitiveness. When Kenny got into that kind of zone, trying to get people to play the way he did, he was a monster. He had three interceptions that game as we recorded the first of back-to-back shutouts.

There was a point when you felt like, "I can't let Kenny down." You knew he wasn't going to let them score, so it was on you to do your part.

Kenny set the tone on and off the field. If he was up and played well, the entire defense usually played well. And in the meetings, if he was in a good mood, the meeting was good and upbeat. But if he wasn't, it was a dark, gloomy room.

When he wanted to, Kenny could be the most engaging, heartfelt guy you could ever meet. But on the flip side, he could be a cold, mean football player. He could be intimidating on or off the field.

Kenny was a guy who could live on four hours of sleep. Some people defy nature that way, and Kenny was one of those special people.

When we were in Cheney for training camp, he would routinely get up at 5:30 AM and go play golf before the first practice. Sometimes he would ask me to come with him. It always sounded good the night before, but when 5:30 came, I would be regretting that I said yes. But there was no way out because Kenny would be there, pounding on my door until I got up. I would be dragging through practice, but he wouldn't miss a beat because that was his routine.

Golf was one of our passions. After the 1987 season, we were down in Palm Springs playing golf. Normally, we'd get up early, hit balls for a couple of hours, go play 18 holes, go hit balls for a couple hours, go play 18 more holes, and, if there was any light left, we'd go hit some more.

We had just finished playing 18 holes, and a couple of PGA pros, Billy Andrade and Jeff Sluman, were up for a round. So I said to Kenny, "Hey, I've got a game with these guys. You and me—let's go." And, to my shock, Kenny replied, "Nah, I'm tired. I want to rest."

I said, "What? Are you kidding?"

I wasn't about to give up a chance to play with some pros, so I went and played, and when I came back, I asked the bartender where Kenny had gone. He said, "He's been in the back of the bar sleeping the whole time." And, sure enough, I found Kenny asleep in a chair with his head down on a table.

I asked him what was going on, and he said he was just tired. Rather than go out that night, he just went up to his room and went to sleep.

The next day, we were out golfing again, and he told me, "I'm seeing some red spots." I kind of laughed at him, but I could see how serious he was. Something definitely wasn't right.

Not too long after we got back home, he called me and said he had been traded to the Phoenix Cardinals. It was very surreal: one of my best friends, the guy I played behind, was getting traded. It wasn't a complete shock because there had been rumors, but I couldn't believe the Seahawks were about to trade the best safety ever to play the game when he was still in his prime. At least, I thought he was still in his prime.

He flew to Arizona to take a physical, and the doctors ended up taking two blood tests because there were some things that were a little disturbing in the first set. Turns out he had almost complete kidney failure.

One part of the physical exam involved running on an inclined treadmill, which got steeper every three minutes. He did it for about 20 minutes, which was the equivalent of running a marathon. And he did it with failing kidneys.

The amazing thing about it was: here's a guy who had just played the 1987 football season—maybe not to where he was before but still at a pretty high level. I remember the coaches were frustrated because he couldn't quite do some things he normally could. He was still playing very well, just not to the standard he had set as one of the best defenders in the league. We knew he had played that year with turf toe, then it turns out he also had been playing with almost complete kidney failure. So when people say he's not a Hall of Famer, my response is: "Are you kidding me?" This guy was a special athlete, and anyone who played with or against him will say he was the greatest safety who ever played the game.

The Seahawks tried to trade Kenny because they thought he was declining in ability and they wanted to get some trade value. They thought they needed to find an eventual replacement for Dave Krieg, and they saw Kelly Stouffer as a potential franchise player. They ended up trading draft picks, including a first-rounder, for Stouffer.

In 1990, when I became a coach, team president Tom Flores said, "Look, you and Kenny are good friends. We have litigation going on right now." I had to guarantee that I would not repeat anything I heard because Kenny and the team were involved in a lawsuit over the cause of his kidney failure. Kenny also had owned a sports agency, and his firm had represented me through my last contract, so that made it a little sensitive, too.

There were hard feelings on both sides for many years. Eventually, the team wanted to embrace Kenny again. They repeatedly asked him to be inducted into the Ring of Honor, but he kept declining. Kenny was very hurt by the previous front office. He just wasn't ready.

But his friends and family really wanted him to do it, and the Seahawks had a new management group, so he finally agreed. And once he was inducted in 2002, I know he was glad he did it.

When he came to Seattle for the ceremony, he was the guest speaker at the Pete Gross Luncheon, and Wyman recalled that Easley talked about how excited he was to be inducted into the Ring of Honor and that he was over the bad blood with the Seahawks. He said he was over it, and he said he was over it, and he said he was over it. And the guy next to Dave Wyman said, "I don't think he's over it."

Whether he is or not, he's where he belongs, recognized among the Seahawks' best players ever. And if Hall of Fame voters are smart, someday he'll be recognized as one of the best NFL players ever, too.

The Boz

The day of my graduation from Stanford, I (Wyman) was reading the newspaper, and I casually flipped to the last page of the sports section and read, "Seahawks Get Bosworth." It totally ruined what should have been a very special day for me.

Bosworth was kind of my nemesis during college because I was an All-American during my senior year, and I was up for the Butkus Award just like he was. But there was always talk about how Bosworth was untouchable, and that he was like no other player. I did admire him, though, and used to look for his highlights on ESPN.

Bosworth came in to be the Seahawks' first celebrity superstar. We had Kenny Easley and Steve Largent, who were the best at their positions in the league. But we never had a star like Boz, who transcended football and was supposed to give the Seahawks some national exposure.

When the Seahawks finally signed him (to a record $11 million over 10 years), they made him my roommate. I think the coaches thought we would probably be starting side by side eventually and that we should get to know each other. But to me, it was a slap in the face. I came to be known as "the Boz's roommate," and no one ever came by our room until Brian finally arrived. Then all of the sudden it was like Grand Central Station. Players like Mike Tice, who hadn't given me the time of day, were coming by our room and kissing his butt.

Brian Bosworth was a great guy. We almost instantly hit it off. But the Boz was another story. I think I was probably the worst person for him in that regard because I was totally intolerant of all that Boz crap. One time before a game, he asked me to help him take out one of his earrings. I looked at him and said, "No, I'm not going to help you take out your earrings, *Brian*. You're a man, and this is *football!*"

Like I said, there was Brian, and then there was the Boz.
Brian would give you a ride to the airport and bring you things. The Boz expected you to do everything for him.
Brian would tell you how much he loved football.

Brian Bosworth struts in his jersey No. 44, two days after receiving a temporary restraining order in King County Superior Court. The NFL says linebackers must wear a number in the 50s or 90s.
Courtesy AP/Wide World Photos

The Boz would say, "I'm going to make my money and get the hell out of this game."

Brian would sign autographs and go visit sick kids in the hospital.

The Boz would push through a crowd and tell people to leave him alone.

Brian was a great businessman and very savvy, whereas I was very naïve and still thought of football as just a game.

In 1987, when we opened up in Denver, I was sitting in the locker room next to Brian when the entire offensive line came strolling in with "Boz Buster" T-shirts. They had gone out to one of the concession stands and purchased the shirts and came sporting them right in front of Brian's locker. Offensive tackle Mike Wilson dropped one on his bench and said, "Here, Boz, we got one for you, too." I remember thinking, "How can you guys be that disloyal?"

After they passed by, I looked at Brian, who was chuckling to himself. "What's so funny?" I asked. "I made those shirts!" he said, still laughing. "Those guys just bought me seat covers for my Corvette!" Sure enough, I inspected the tag and it read: "44 Boz Inc."—Brian's company.

I was very loyal to Brian and protective of him whenever people criticized him. To this day, I defend him when people say he never did anything on the field. His rookie year, he played really well and made the NFL all-rookie team. But when he would break into his Boz character, I could very easily chastise him. One time during an interview, the Boz was whining about the fans in Seattle: "They've built a ladder so high for me, I'll never be able to climb it." I told him, "Brian, you built the ladder and got paid $11 million to build it!"

His rookie year, I (Moyer) belonged to Sand Point Country Club, and a lot of members wanted me to bring the Boz. So I asked him if he wanted to go golfing, and he said, "Yeah." He showed up with short shorts and a short-sleeved shirt that was unbuttoned all the way down—not acceptable golfing attire for a private club. But no one seemed to make a big deal of it, so we went and played.

Every other hole, whether Brian hit the fairway or not, we couldn't find his golf ball. About the 6th hole, we figured out why: people were coming through the trees and stealing his golf balls. By the 9th hole, word had gotten out that the Boz was there, and we had a gallery following us.

Afterward, I got a letter from the country club that said, "If you ever invite Brian Bosworth again, we'd like you to make sure he has proper attire. Meanwhile, we're putting you on probation for three months."

I just thought, "You've got to be kidding. You guys begged me to get him out there, and now I'm on probation."

In Newport in 1988, we (Wyman, Boz, some other guys, and I) all went out. I was the poorest of the group even though I was the most veteran guy. And they were ordering all of this food and drink. At one point, Boz got up to go to the bathroom. Then Wyman went to the bathroom, and somebody else went to the bathroom. Next thing I know, they're outside the window laughing at me because they had stiffed me with the bill. While Boz was a good businessman, he also was, as Chuck Knox would say, a cheap prick.

Because of who he was, Brian didn't have to play by the rules. When you were with the Boz, you got free drinks and free food and could cut to the front of every line. It was great for me (Wyman) because nobody even looked at me, which is just what I wanted.

He was like a rock star everywhere he went, especially when we were on the road. And that's why he originally wanted to play for a team like New York, Chicago, or Los Angeles. In Seattle, people didn't treat him that way. One time I walked into the Central Tavern in Kirkland with him, and everyone at the bar turned and looked at us. With his colored Mohawk and earrings, he was probably one of the most recognizable people in the country, but everyone just turned right back around and went back to drinking his or her beer.

After the Boz had worn out his welcome in Seattle, people really turned on him. Brian and I were out to dinner with a bunch of people one time, and some autograph seekers came over to our table. Just as Brian started to transform himself into the Boz, they reached past him and said, "Mr. Wyman, we think you are a great linebacker. Will you sign this?" I remember thinking that should have been a good moment for me, but because of my loyalty to Brian, it was very uncomfortable.

It's weird to hang out with someone who has that kind of celebrity status. Curt Warner had that, and we (Warner and Moyer) were best friends. It was almost like you became their caddie or sidekick. No one ever talked to you. They wanted to talk to them. And you'd be like, "Let's go. Let's wrap this thing up and get out of here." It's very weird to be around people like that.

That's what it often was like to hang out with the character known as the Boz, who wasn't as much fun to know or spend time with as the regular guy known as Brian Bosworth.

chapter 4
1988

Curt Warner and his teammates were finally able to top the Chargers and the rest of the competitive AFC West to become champs of the division in 1988.

The First Division Title

The 1988 season opener against Denver was my (Wyman's) first game as a starter in the NFL, and, boy, was I nervous. All I could get down in a pregame meal was a bowl of Froot Loops and some grapes, and I threw it all up into a garbage can just before kickoff. I remember Brian Bosworth, who had started as a rookie in 1987, sitting next to me, going, "Take it easy. Calm down. You'll be okay."

On the second series, I had a colossal collision with tight end Clarence Kay. I met him at the line of scrimmage and jammed his head with a forearm rip, and he went straight down. It stunned me, and I fell, too. Joe Nash had knifed through and made Tony Dorsett fumble, and the ball one-hopped right into my hands as I hit the ground.

I came over to the sideline and was kind of dazed. I wasn't aware of how hard the collision had been, but there was blood down the front of my jersey from a big gash on my chin. As they stapled it shut, I sat there feeling like I had gotten my ass kicked. Not knowing what was going on out on the field and still a little dazed, I looked at trainer John Kasik and said, "I think that dude knocked the crap out of me." Kasik replied, "You're sure a lot better off than he is." I looked out on the field and saw they were taking Kay off on a stretcher. Someone told me his legs weren't moving, but later in the game I spotted him standing on the sideline in his street clothes.

We also lost Steve Largent in that game. I remember being right there, watching him getting laid out by Denver safety Mike Harden. It was a nasty hit. Afterward, Harden got up and celebrated in a way that seemed to channel the frustration of every defensive back who was 10 times faster than Steve and a better athlete than Steve but had gotten burned by him a million times.

It was a hard-hitting game, and we went up there and stood toe to toe with them and punched them in the mouth, beating them 21–14.

I (Moyer) knew we were going to win. They couldn't do much against us that day. We played at a high level and were very determined to prove that we were the team to beat in the AFC West that year. It's hard to go on the road and win, especially in Denver, where we hadn't had a lot of success, but we knew it was our year.

We won the next week at home against Kansas City, too. Jacob Green had a big game, we got six turnovers, and won 31–10.

The next week at San Diego, we blew that game. That was the game in which Dave got hurt. His shoulder was separated when he was driven into the hard dirt infield at Jack Murphy Stadium. The Chargers won 17–6. And Jeff Kemp suddenly became our quarterback. Defensively, we played pretty well, and it was our third game in a row keeping our opponents to 17 points or less. So confidence on the defensive side of the ball was still high going into our next game against the San Francisco 49ers.

Before that game, Tom Catlin stood up and said, "We're playing the 49ers. This will be a great test. You've got the number-one offense in the NFL [the 49ers] against the number-two defense [us]."

We were pretty excited. They had Joe Montana, Roger Craig, Jerry Rice. This team was loaded. We knew they were good.

That day they were too good. They beat us 38–7. And it wasn't that close. I'm surprised we gave up only 38. Seems like it was 55. When we were done with that game, they were still the number-one offense in the NFL, but we were about 28th in defense. They had 580 yards—more than I (Moyer) can ever remember giving up in a game.

I (Wyman) had 16 tackles in that game and was the league's top tackler that week. Everyone was calling to tell me congratulations, and I told them, "I had the worst game you could possibly have." It was just because there were lots of tackles to be had. I probably missed 16 tackles, too.

The next week, we went to Atlanta and played in front of 28,000 people. We won 31–20 with Kelly Stouffer at quarterback, replacing Kemp. And Stouffer played pretty decently. John L. Williams scored three touchdowns in that game.

We went to Cleveland the next week, and I (Moyer) saved the game by unintentionally putting the Browns' quarterback out. We blocked a field goal, I picked the ball up in mid-stride, and was running down the sideline when the ball started to come loose. I had to slow down to secure it, and that allowed Mike Pagel, the Browns' quarterback and field-goal holder, to catch up to me. He caught me at the 10-yard line after I had run 67 yards. When he tackled me, I ended up driving him into the turf, and he separated his shoulder.

We only got a field goal out of it, but it was worth it because we put their number-one quarterback out. I don't remember who came in next, but he wasn't very good. We beat them 16–10.

Then we played New Orleans, which was a very good team that year. They had Bobby Hebert at quarterback and those great linebackers—Rickey Jackson, Pat Swilling, Sam Mills, and Vaughan Johnson—and beat us 20–19 for their sixth win in a row on the way to the NFC West title. Meanwhile, we dropped to 4–3 as we headed to Los Angeles to play the Rams.

I (Moyer) grew up in Orange County, Southern California, so all of my family and friends were there to watch me for the first time as a pro starter. The Rams played their games at Anaheim Stadium, which was just 10 miles from where I grew up.

But I didn't play well. I got beat for a touchdown for the first time I could remember, and I didn't make many tackles. The one bright spot: I helped us score our only touchdown when we blocked a field goal. I recovered and flipped the ball to Melvin Jenkins, who scored. But it was a bad day. Jim Everett threw for 311 yards and three touchdowns, and they blew us out 31–10.

We went back home and beat San Diego 17–14 and then lost in the Kingdome, 13–3, to a Buffalo team that had the best pass-rushing defense in the league with Bruce Smith, Cornelius Bennett, and those guys. Chuck Knox gave a memorable pregame speech the night before, which we talk about earlier in this book.

We went 3–4 while Krieg was out that year. We were just trying to hang on until he returned, and we knew we were still in it when he came back for the Houston game the next week. We had three huge defensive plays in that game. We stopped them on fourth-and-one late in the game. Moyer intercepted a pass in the end zone, and Wyman recovered a fumble to help us set up the last drive. Then Krieg led us to a last-second field goal as we beat Warren Moon and the Oilers 27–24. That was a big win for us because Houston was a playoff team and a Super Bowl contender.

That put us over .500 again as we went to Kansas City, and for the first time in a long time we had a chance to win there. We were better than they were (they were 4–11–1 that year), and it was one of the few times we actually played a good game at Arrowhead Stadium. But we still didn't make enough plays at the end of the game, and we lost 27–24. That was the eighth straight loss by the Seahawks in Kansas City, and I (Moyer) had played in six of those.

The next week, we played the Raiders at the Kingdome on *Monday Night Football*. We had been embarrassed the year before on *MNF* by Bo Jackson, who had run for more than 200 yards and plowed through Brian Bosworth on that infamous short touchdown run. We were determined not to let him run all over us again, and we did a good job on him. We held the Raiders to 257 total yards and forced two turnovers, but they were in the game because our offense turned the ball over five times.

But the offense overcame the turnovers as Krieg threw five touchdown passes, and Curt Warner and John L. Williams both rushed for 100 yards. That was the first time we had ever had two guys go over 100 in the same game. We beat the Raiders 35–27 in front of one of the best, loudest crowds we ever had at the Kingdome.

The next week in New England was the coldest game we've ever played in, and we lost to the Patriots 13–7. It was windy, too, so the wind-chill factor that day was minus-10. Because of that, they didn't throw the ball very much. There were 67 defensive plays, and I (Wyman) swear their right guard, Sean Farrell, and I must have head-butted each other on 50 of those plays. We would look at each other before every play like, "Here we go again!" I was glad it was cold because it helped slow down the swelling that was occurring around my brain.

Doug Flutie could not throw the ball over 20 yards because the wind was blowing so hard. It became three downs and a cloud of white snow. We knew it was going to be one of those hard-fought games, and whoever wanted it most was going to win it. We should have shut them out; they didn't have a very good offense that year.

After losing in New England, we were 7–7 with two games left, against Denver and in Los Angeles. Curt Warner ran for 126 yards and four touchdowns as we beat the Broncos 42–14 in the Kingdome and swept the season series for just the second time. We were determined not to let the Broncos win the West that year.

That was the game where Largent got even with Harden for the hit in the opener. Harden intercepted a pass by Krieg and was running it back when Largent tracked him down and leveled him. He nearly bent Harden in half, and although Harden's hit on Steve had been more vicious, Steve's hit almost felt just. It was as if good was on his side. For Steve to get vindication the way he did, it was like a storybook tale.

His reaction to the hit was classic, too. He hesitated for a moment as if he were about to celebrate but then realized, "Hey, there's a football lying on the ground…I'd better jump on it first!" At that moment, the noise in the Kingdome was ear-splitting; everyone was thrilled to see Largent exact revenge the way he did. I'll never forget that hit, and I doubt anyone else who saw it will, either.

Then we went to L.A. to play the Raiders in the season finale. The winner would win the AFC West; the loser would go home. Certainly a dream game.

Krieg had another great game, throwing for 410 yards and four touchdowns, and John L. had 180 receiving yards. He saved us with a 75-yard touchdown off a backside screen pass.

Every time I (Moyer) thought we had the game won, they would air one out. It was like the NFL gods said, "Hey, we're going to have a barn-burner today." We were up by 13 late in the game, but Terry Taylor gave up a long touchdown. They were just airing it. It was a free-for-all.

It was horrible, too, because I was the one who gave the motivational speech the night before, and then we gave up 37 points. We were fired up and ready to play, and then we gave up 37 points. I never gave a motivational speech again.

We were ahead 43–37, and on the final play the Raiders threw a Hail Mary. They had Willie Gault, an Olympic sprinter and great high jumper. I was behind him, and I knew I couldn't outjump him, so I stepped on his right foot and grabbed his pants, pulling him down so he couldn't jump up and get the ball. He was *not* going to get up and get that ball.

We almost lost that game on a Hail Mary. It was a huge monkey off our back because we never had won the West. We never had had a bye going into the playoffs.

We played Cincinnati in the playoffs, and they had the best offense in the NFL that year. Chuck made us believe we were going to beat Cincinnati, and he had a unique plan for doing it.

We couldn't practice at the stadium the day before the game because they had the tarp on it to keep the snow off. Chuck said, "Screw them. We're going to kick their butts, anyway." He used that as a motivator. And we should have won.

We had put together a strategy to slow down the Bengals' no-huddle offense. If Chuck raised one hand, nose tackle Joe Nash was supposed to fake an injury. If two, it was defensive end Jeff Bryant.

Well, Boogie was a first-rounder and one of Chuck's favorites, while Joe was an expendable undrafted free agent. So the joke was that Chuck just couldn't get his other arm up there, so it was always Joe. He knew Joe could take it, while Boogie was Chuck's boy and Chuck didn't want to embarrass him like that.

So Joe ended up taking a dive several times in that game. The best one was when Joe fell down on the wrong side of the line of scrimmage. He was supposed to fall on their side of the line to slow down their offense. But as he started to go down, the ref moved the ball, so there Joe was, limping with his fake injury to get to the other side of the ball. Poor Joe. It was one of the great sacrifices by the player who would set the franchise record for games played (218).

The Cincinnati players were quite outraged that we had found a way to cheat, too. They were really giving Nash a bunch of crap about it because it was obvious the whole thing was contrived. They were all over Joe, which I'm sure was really hard for him to take.

On one play, I (Wyman) got hit in the balls. I went down and was really suffering, but Chuck must not have noticed it because he put his arm up...and Joe went down right next to me.

One of the Bengals complained to the ref, "Oh, now they're both doing it!" I responded in my new high-pitched voice, "No, I'm really hurt!"

It was pretty smart of Chuck, though. He was the only one who came up with a way to slow down that offense that year. If they started to substitute and you ran your guys out there to match them, they would run back off and snap the ball. Now they don't allow that. You can't have 12 guys in the huddle.

They were running all over us in the first half, so we went in at halftime and switched from our traditional 3-4 defense to a 4-3. It was a brilliant strategy. We shut them out in the second half, holding them to just 116 yards, and gave our team a chance to win the game. But we turned the ball over twice on offense inside their 5-yard line and missed an extra point. We should have won that game.

It was a fun year, a good group of guys. It did feel like that was the beginning of the end. Largent probably should have retired in 1988. They were always trying to get rid of Krieg. Curt Warner had slowed down. Kenny Easley was already gone. Jacob Green was getting older. We were a team that needed to get younger.

Ken Behring

The Nordstroms sold the Seahawks to Ken Behring in 1988, and the feeling around the organization immediately changed.

It was out with Wall Street, in with Club Med. It became less a business and more like a social club.

John Nordstrom was a classy guy who was respected immensely by all the players. He was rarely seen, except when we won a big game. He let the football people run the team. John Nordstrom was the epitome of class.

It was quite a contrast to Behring, a California real-estate baron who came across as a used-car salesman. He was just the most uncharismatic owner. Usually, people with that kind of money who have achieved that status have some kind of presence. But Behring was like a lottery winner. And he was always dressed so sloppily—sansabelt slacks and a Seahawks T-shirt. It was just the worst image for an NFL owner.

While the Nordstroms shunned the spotlight, Behring sought it out.

In one of his first public appearances, he grabbed a bunch of SeaGals and had his picture taken with them. It's not something you ever would have seen John Nordstrom do, so it was kind of surprising to see the new owner do it.

Behring always had an entourage of guys with slicked-back hair and trench coats, and we all asked, "Who are these guys?"

One of them was a guy named Mike Blatt. He had been the agent for quarterback Kelly Stouffer when the Seahawks got Stouffer in a trade with the Phoenix Cardinals in April 1988. Then Blatt had helped broker the sale of the team from the Nordstroms to the Behrings that year.

When the Seahawks fired general manager Mike McCormack after the 1988 season, Blatt was Seattle's GM for three weeks until they hired Tom Flores. A few months later, Blatt was charged with setting up the murder of a business associate in California. He was tried twice for the crime, but both times he avoided a conviction because of a hung jury.

That tells you a little bit about the kind of people Behring surrounded himself with. It wasn't that he was a bad guy or ever did anything illegal, but the feeling around the team was quite different.

Behring treated the team like it was a toy. He would invite his entourage to come meet players and the SeaGals.

Behring Was Shaky as a Public Speaker

If you ever sat down with him and talked real estate, Ken Behring sounded very intelligent. He was very confident and engaging.

He also was renowned as a world-class hunter; it was one of his passions. One time some of the coaches flew on the team plane with him to Key West, and he brought out all of his expensive hunting guns and showed us this grizzly head that supposedly was the largest ever claimed on a hunt. He just lit up as he told stories about his hunting.

When he was not in his world, however, Behring was almost timid and shy and had a hard time communicating with people.

In 1992, when we had the worst offense in NFL history, he came into the locker room before the Raiders game and tried to give us a pep talk. His voice started shaking, and cornerback Brian Davis turned to me (Wyman) and said, "He sounds like Katharine Hepburn." And he did. He sounded exactly like the old Katharine Hepburn. And then I spent the rest of his speech trying not to laugh.

But it was so bizarre. He said, voice shaking à la Hepburn, "Oh, I don't like the Raiders, and I know you guys don't like them."

Some guys will want to stand up in a meeting, and every once in a while, you think, "Just let him finish," because you know he's not going to say anything inspiring or meaningful at all. In this instance, it was shocking, and all I could think was, "We're dead."

His intentions were good. He obviously wanted us to beat the Raiders. But he was extremely nervous, and it came across quite poorly.

He lost all credibility as a speaker that day. One, he was not a very good speaker, so he wasn't naturally motivational. But he also said, "We have the talent in this room." And I (Moyer) was thinking, "There's not one person in this room who believes our offense has the talent to win." So you can't say things like that. You have to be truthful and honest about it.

Football Fools

Ken and David Behring were very nice people. But they just knew nothing about football.

Again, it was like Ken thought the team was a toy. For the football people, it was serious business, and we didn't feel they were treating it the same way.

Ken fired Mike McCormack and hired Tom Flores because, as Ken said, "Tom Flores shares my football philosophy." And we just thought, "What philosophy, Ken? You don't have a football philosophy." But that didn't stop him from making the call on drafting quarterback Dan McGwire in the first round in 1991. It was a move that upset Chuck Knox, who refused to play Stouffer or McGwire that year.

Chuck said, "I never rebuild. When you rebuild, you rebuild for someone else." And Flores found that out when he was fired after the 1994 season.

If Ken Behring was really trying to run it like a team, he would have put football people in charge. Instead, it was, "I'm going to hire my buddies, and I'm going to hire my son."

David Behring convinced his dad that he could run the team, so he replaced Flores as team president. He wanted it to be a career, and he really got into it. But he wasn't prepared to be the president. From passion and love of the Seahawks, he had what was needed. From an experience standpoint in the NFL, he wasn't ready.

Because of their inexperience, the Behrings were easily influenced. I (Moyer) didn't know how to play the political game; I was too young. But some of the other coaches knew how to play the game.

So did Randy Mueller. He was in David Behring's ear. How does someone go from ball boy to player personnel to running the organization as quickly as Mueller did? It's not a knock on Mueller—Randy's very talented—but it shows that the Behrings didn't know how to run an organization.

All of a sudden, people were leap-frogging into positions without going through the standard steps to get there. They went from Mike McCormack and Chuck Knox to David Behring and Dennis Erickson. Look at how they hired those guys. It wasn't the way it was—or is—done in the NFL. No one feared this organization.

In 1992 we had the worst offense in the history of the NFL, and yet they kept all of the offensive coaches for the next season.

When Erickson got there in 1995, they kept three of the coaches from the worst offense in NFL history. It was more of a buddy system than a merit system.

Poor Decisions

When the Behrings hired Erickson in 1995, they didn't go through a thorough interview process. Erickson was at the University of Miami, but Miami was rumored to be going on probation, so he took the Seahawks job when the Behrings offered it.

They offered him the job *over the phone*. You run a multimillion-dollar organization and are looking for someone to head your franchise, and you don't spend quality interview time with the guy? You don't sit down with him and find out what his philosophy is? You don't do a thorough background check?

There were plenty of rumors about Erickson's drinking and lack of discipline from his football teams at the University of Miami.

And that came back to bite them pretty quickly because three months after he was hired, Erickson got pulled over for DUI near his hometown of Everett, Washington. He reportedly blew a .23 (percent blood-alcohol level), and they said you could follow his route by the trail of 911 calls from people who called to tell the state patrol to get him off the road.

That was the first sign that the Behrings had made a poor decision. When you're a 48-year-old man and a leader of men, you can't make those kinds of poor decisions. That doesn't mean Erickson was a bad guy, but his decision-making certainly had to be in question.

Chuck Knox liked to have a good time, but he never made poor decisions like that. When he had been drinking, he always had a driver. He knew the importance of his role as a leader.

Dennis was not liked by a lot of people in the Seahawks organization. He was not respected by everyone because he didn't treat some people well. He was rude to doctors, media, subordinates, and others at times. Some people say the class of an organization is reflected in how people are treated from the top down. You treat the president of the company with the same respect as the person who takes out the garbage. Every person in the organization is important. Dennis didn't treat everyone with respect.

Dennis was notorious for challenging team doctors when they would say a player was injured. He was paranoid and would accuse them of trying to get him fired. He accused me (Moyer) of trying to get him fired when I had my radio show. It was just bizarre. He said I mentioned on the air that the Seahawks should fire him.

What I said was, "He's a big boy, and he knows this year [1998] is a critical year for him. If he doesn't make the playoffs, there is a chance they will fire him."

I've been a coach, so I know how sensitive being under scrutiny can be, and I would never call for another coach to be fired. The ironic thing was the other 700 hours I was on the air I was always defending him, and people called me a "homer" for defending him. But insecurity drives people to say strange things.

His paranoia led to blaming other people for his failures. "I got fired because of you. We missed the playoffs because of that call in the Jets game."

They had three games left. They played 13 games before that. But that one call (Vinny Testaverde's bogus touchdown) cost them the playoffs?

Yeah, that was a horrible call—and it led to the return of instant replay—and I have empathy for the team because I've lost games on bad calls before. But Dennis was not fired because of that call; it was because he never had a winning record. The Seahawks were 31–33 and never went to the playoffs in his four years coaching the team.

Paul Allen bought the team in June 1997, and he essentially gave Erickson two years to prove what kind of man and coach he was, and getting to the playoffs certainly wouldn't have hurt his cause. But when he couldn't do it, Allen fired him and brought in Mike Holmgren.

That was the end of a forgettable decade in Seahawks history. Allen and Holmgren eventually made the Seahawks the model, respectable franchise it had been before the Nordstroms sold it to Ken Behring.

chapter 5
The Quarterbacks

Dave Krieg was a competitor and a control freak—winning traits for an NFL quarterback.

Dave Krieg

Everybody loved Dave Krieg. But as much fun as he was, he was also a pain in the butt. And we mean that in the best way possible.

Dave was like a girlfriend who wants constant affection and praise. Every once in a while, you just want to sit on the couch and watch TV, but she won't let you. Dave was just like that.

If there's one word that describes Dave, it's *competitive*.

He was the ultimate competitor. He was always bored and always had to have something to do. He was always moving, always grabbing people to do something with him because he was a guy who didn't like to be alone.

He was a control freak, because you had to do it his way when it was his idea. Sometimes you'd just have to stop him and say, "Dave, this isn't a football field; you're not the quarterback here."

But he made it so much fun that people couldn't help but go along. Dave would make it worth your while for you to go hang out with him, offering to pay for dinner or buy the beer. He would make everything sound like it was going to be exciting.

One time, he wanted me (Moyer) to go to Olympia with him to pick up something for his boat. He didn't want to drive to Olympia by himself. Somehow he convinced me what a great time we would have driving two hours round trip, so I went with him.

Home-Field Advantage

He couldn't go out very often because he had a family, so he would invite people over so he would have somebody to compete against. You'd play golf all day, might go bowling, then go back to his house and play cribbage and pool into the wee hours of the night.

One time I (Wyman) walked into his house, and he had all of the furniture pushed to the side. On one end of the room was a five-foot high plastic basketball hoop. On the other end was Dave shooting jumpers with a little rubber ball. His wife, Sue, was standing next to the backboard so she could rebound. And his young sons were on the side looking kind of longingly, as if to say, "When can we play, Dad?" And, of course, the answer was, "Not until I make 20 in a row."

He got to 18 and then missed. So we all had to wait until he made 20 before we finally got to eat. Then the games started up again after dinner. And God forbid anyone but Dave would win because then you were in for a late night—Dave wasn't going to quit until he had won. In the wee hours, Sue would come downstairs and give me a look like it was time to go, so I would begin to slough off cards. Then it was, "Oh, darn, I didn't see those points. You win, Dave. Good night!"

Dave was a very good pool player. I (Moyer) decided I wouldn't play him until I was good enough to win. So I bought a pool table and practiced for three months.

Dave invited me over for one of our competitive game nights. We started with cribbage. We were playing for a buck a point, and I somehow managed to skunk him one time, which is a big deal in the world of cribbage.

Then we went downstairs to play pool, and it was always double or nothing. We played until 4:00 in the morning, and he couldn't understand how I was beating him because I had never beaten him before. What he didn't know was that I had been practicing for three months.

He accused me of cheating and moving the balls. He came back from the bathroom and said, "That's not how they were set up."

I said, "I can't help you now, Dave. You've now lost to me so much you're accusing me of cheating at pool."

This is the guy who needed to win so badly he would even cheat at Pictionary—against our wives. Dave, Wyman, and I were playing the game against our wives one night, and Dave Krieg actually wrote down the word. My wife saw me try to stifle a laugh, and she looked over and couldn't believe Dave was cheating at Pictionary.

After the 1988 playoffs, Dave Krieg and Wyman were playing pool against me and tight end John Spagnola. Wyman was just having a good time with it, and whenever it was his turn, he would say, "Well, let's see if I can't make this shot."

And Krieg would jump in and say, "No, Wyman, see if you *can* make it!"

He was just such a positive thinker. And so competitive at the same time. As usual, we were playing double or nothing that night, and the stakes had climbed into the thousands of dollars. Not that anyone would ever pay that much, but it seemed to heighten the tension and bring out everyone's competitive spirit.

The Daves had won 11 games in a row, Wyman had a shot on the eight ball for win number 12, and Krieg told him, "This is a tough shot. Whatever you do, don't scratch on the eight ball."

Well, Wyman scratched on the eight ball, and Spagnola and I won. And Krieg was all over Wyman: "Noooo! I told you not to scratch the eight ball! I knew you were going to do that!"

And that's when you'd have to remind Krieg once more that they didn't have quarterbacks in pool, either.

A Leader on the Field, Not Always Off

But it was that competitiveness that made him a really good leader on the football field.

He was very good about including everybody. We had such a good, tight-knit group and guys from very diverse backgrounds. It didn't matter where you were from, Dave always included everybody and invited everybody. And in that respect he was a really good leader by example. He didn't say a lot. But his competitiveness at practice, it was like a game.

You wonder how it is that he's a leader if he doesn't say anything. But after a whole season of being with him and his displaying that character, it kind of grows on the team.

He was definitely more of a leader by example, though. He liked to talk, but he wasn't the best communicator. He certainly wasn't much of a motivational speaker. He wasn't very tactful, and his message didn't always come across the way he intended.

Kenny Easley once got a personal foul that played a part in us losing a game, and on the flight back Dave told Kenny he had made a dumb play, insinuating that it had cost us the game. Kenny, a very talented and prideful player who already was upset about it, got very emotional and broke down right there on the plane. Dave made probably the toughest guy on our team cry.

On another flight, coming back from a preseason game in Japan in 1990, Dave decided to be the quarterback of Joe Nash's life. He told Nash's wife, Nancy, that she needed to move from Boston out to Seattle during the season to support Joe. He basically criticized her for not supporting Joe and kept going on about it until finally Nancy cursed at him and stormed off to another part of the plane.

Dave would say what was on his mind. Some people would think it, but Dave would actually say it. He didn't have much tact or diplomacy.

There's not one person that Dave hasn't ticked off at some point. But there also isn't a single person who hasn't had a good time with him.

And you never could stay mad at him for long. Just ask Nancy Nash. Dave felt so bad about harassing her that he sent her flowers.

Benched or Beaten, Krieg Kept Coming Back for More

Dave Krieg's mental toughness was amazing. Dave could screw the pooch like nobody. But he never let it bother him. He would get back in the huddle and say, "Okay, let's make that work."

In Atlanta in 1991, Krieg had one of his passes picked off by Deion Sanders. Everybody else put their heads down and walked off the field because, once Deion caught the ball, it was over. Within two steps. I (Wyman) was standing there as he went past me, and his feet were touching the ground about once every eight yards. He was like a deer, just prancing by, and doing his high step.

I looked back toward the field, and here came Dave Krieg. Whereas Deion was barely touching the ground, Dave was chewing up the turf running as hard as he could. You know when you're a little kid and you try to show your parents you're running real hard, so you flail your arms as you go? That's what Dave looked like.

I just looked at him like, "Dave, what are you doing?" Then at the 20-yard line, he made a futile dive. And I thought, "Come on, you're embarrassing yourself."

But he was so competitive. He would never give up, and he always thought there was a way to win.

The one play that defines Dave Krieg so well was that Kansas City game in 1990, when he ducked the eighth sack by Derrick Thomas and threw the winning touchdown pass to Paul Skansi. I think people take that for granted, but if you think about getting sacked that many times—the same guy hitting you that many times—it would have to get discouraging. After a while, you would have to think, "Okay, here it comes again." Your psyche as a human being would cause you to think, "This is the part where I fall on the ground because I'm going to get hit in the back again."

But that was Dave, to say, "Nope, you're not going to get me this time."

As a team, we had confidence that we had a chance to win every game. Krieg may get hot. There also was a chance that he may do something to hurt you—the ball slips out of his hand or he runs down the sideline even though he's not in uniform and gets a 15-yard penalty as we are about to kick a field goal and tie it up (he did this in a game against New Orleans in 1991). But we always felt we had a chance to win.

Dave was inconsistent at times and got benched a lot during his career, but when they put in Jeff Kemp, Sean Salisbury, or Kelly Stouffer, we never felt we had as good a chance to win as when Dave was in there. Even when he was on a cold streak, you thought your best chance to win was with Dave.

He deserved whatever credit he got because he didn't get very much of it, but he didn't deserve all of the criticism. He might be the most underappreciated quarterback in NFL history. Teammates had a completely different perception of him than fans did.

The Seahawks were always trying to bring someone in to replace Dave Krieg. And he outlasted all of the guys they brought in to replace him.

And it's all because he was one of the most competitive quarterbacks ever to play in the NFL.

First-Round Flops

The Seattle Seahawks have never drafted a quarterback who has worked out.

In a six-year period from 1988 through 1993, we used first-round picks on Kelly Stouffer, Dan McGwire, and Rick Mirer.

When Stouffer first came here in 1988, everyone thought, "Wow, he has a strong arm!" But by the end of his first year, he couldn't throw a spiral.

Dave Krieg got hurt early in the 1988 season, and Jeff Kemp started against San Francisco. We were blown out by the 49ers 38–7, and our only touchdown came on a pass from Stouffer after he had broken his nose. Curt Warner accidentally bumped into him and knocked him down. But Stouffer got up off the ground and threw a touchdown pass.

Stouffer started the next week at Atlanta, and we won 31–20. In his third start, against New Orleans, he set a team rookie record with 370 passing yards. By the end of the year, though, he could not throw a spiral.

Dan Was Not the Man

We were in the war room when they picked Dan McGwire in the first round in 1991, and it was the first time I (Moyer) ever saw Chuck Knox look defeated. The coaching staff did not want to draft Dan with that pick. They had other quarterbacks, such as Browning Nagle and Brett Favre, rated higher.

When our pick came up, team president Tom Flores motioned to Chuck to leave the war room with him. They went into a private room with owner Ken Behring. Chuck was the first one to come back into the war room. His jaw was clinched, and it was obvious he was not happy with the pick we were about to announce.

We ended up drafting McGwire, and Chuck didn't go down to the media room to announce the pick, as he usually did. He let Behring and Flores do it.

Meanwhile, Chuck motioned for all of the coaches to follow him to our meeting room. And he told us, "Boys, coach your asses off this year because this is the beginning of the end."

He was very upset that Behring and Flores had overruled him on the draft pick, and he knew there was a fundamental difference in philosophy.

Behring and Flores wanted that Oakland Raiders–style, seven-step-drop, strong-armed quarterback. The irony was that McGwire became a first-round prospect that year largely because he almost led his school, San Diego State, to an upset over Miami. And he did it using a *three-step* drop the whole game.

Teams were attracted to McGwire for a lot of reasons. He was a great guy who came from a good family and never got in trouble. He played in a pro-style offense at San Diego State, was accurate, and stood 6'8"—an unprecedented height for an NFL quarterback. He also had a slingshot for an arm, which means he could throw the ball 65–70 yards.

However, a slingshot does not always get the ball there quickly. McGwire had an extremely slow release. In a preseason game in 1991, he went back to pass on the far left hash mark and threw it across the field to the other sideline. The free safety, who was in the middle of the field, saw Dan winding up and had enough time to run all the way to the sideline and intercept it—something that shouldn't happen in the NFL. And I said, "That's not good."

I (Wyman) remember watching him trying to complete a little swing pass to the running back in the flat, and he threw it in the dirt. You could tell he was trying so hard to do it right, but he just wasn't a natural player. He just didn't let it flow, and it's too bad because he was the kind of guy that you would really pull for—a great guy.

I (Moyer) liked Dan, too, and tried to mentor him and give him some confidence. We were playing Dallas in his first regular-season game, and I was talking to him before the game, trying to encourage him and pump him up. He had dry mouth so bad, I knew he was going to have a hard time managing his nerves against one of the best teams in the league. He ended up getting hurt, and Dallas shut us out 27–0.

We kind of saw this coming earlier in the year, right after we had drafted McGwire.

Dave Krieg, myself (Moyer), Rusty Tillman, and McGwire were out golfing. We were paired up, and coming up to the 18th hole we decided to go double or nothing. Just before we got to the green, we doubled it again. Dan had a two-foot putt, and Dave had an eight-footer.

Dave walked up to his ball, glanced at the hole, and drained his putt. At that point, Dan started to get nervous. Then I watched as Dan spent the next 10 minutes walking around the green, fretting about his two-foot putt.

I remember Rusty looking at me, and we both thought the same thing: "Why's this guy worrying over a two-footer for a lousy 20 bucks?"

The old quarterback, on his way out, comes out cold as ice and nails an eight-footer. And our new heir apparent is walking around fretting about a two-footer.

And then the heir apparent missed the putt.

And Rusty said, "Oh, man, we're in trouble."

When Krieg was hurt in 1991, McGwire started against Indianapolis. We were ahead 17–3 at halftime, and Chuck pulled him and put Jeff Kemp back in. And Behring and Flores were very unhappy.

After the game, Chuck said, "Guys, I'm going to take some flak for this. But quite frankly, I'm here to win. I'm not here to play who they want us to play. I thought our best chance was to put Kemp back in the game."

Basically, what he said right there was, "Screw you, Behring."

We Came to Rue Missing Out on Drew

In 1992, if we hadn't beaten New England 10–6 in the third week, we would have gotten Drew Bledsoe in the draft the next year.

That was a course-changing game for the Seahawks. We both finished 2–14. Our other win came in overtime against Denver at home late in the season—an emotional game because Pete Gross, our team broadcaster who had terminal cancer, was inducted into the Ring of Honor beforehand.

So by beating the Patriots and Broncos, we missed out on the number-one pick, which we would have used on Bledsoe, the Washington State star.

Bledsoe is the greatest quarterback I've ever seen on film in college. He had a Dan Marino release with a stronger arm. And Mirer appeared to be just a guy. At Notre Dame, he was a good player. He ran well. He wasn't extremely accurate, didn't have an overly quick release, didn't have an extraordinarily strong arm. You could see on film he was a good player in college. But Drew Bledsoe stood out. You said, "No question. Number-one pick in the draft."

It is quite remarkable that we've never drafted a meaningful quarterback. They've all been free agents or trade guys. There really are only three: Jim Zorn, Dave Krieg, and Matt Hasselbeck.

Jon Kitna was a free agent, Warren Moon was a free agent. Even today, they still haven't drafted a guy who's capable of taking over.

Mirer Couldn't Pass the Test

His rookie year, Mirer was pretty smart. He made some good decisions. He didn't do the typical things that most quarterbacks did in their rookie years. He didn't do anything stupid to screw things up. He was smart that way. I (Wyman) was playing with Denver then, and I got a sack on him because he ran out of bounds behind the line of scrimmage, and I ran him out. He probably should have thrown it away, but at least he didn't throw some crazy pass and have it intercepted.

His rookie year, they decided to keep it really simple. It was a quick progression. One, two, and if it wasn't there, he tucked it and ran. That's what they taught him. And he was good. He scrambled a lot. He never was a real accurate passer—he was

Rick Mirer was one of the Seahawks' high quarterback draft picks that didn't pan out in the late 1980s and early 1990s.
Courtesy AP/Wide World Photos

high on his throws a lot—but he was a good athlete who was capable of winning.

After Mirer's rookie year, we all said, "Hey, we've got a quarterback." We even said he was probably better for us than Bledsoe would have been because we didn't protect the quarterback that well, and Mirer had scrambling ability.

Clearly, by his second and third year, that had changed. It wasn't that he was bad. He just didn't improve. And he wasn't accurate.

I (Moyer) think we all thought we had a quarterback. But it just didn't work. He lost confidence. And when he lost it, he lost it.

As he was asked to do more, actually read defenses, he really struggled with that. And when Dennis Erickson was hired, who knows what Erickson was teaching him? I've heard from many people that Erickson's offense just was not very complex. I don't think anyone was teaching Mirer how to read defenses.

The one thing you don't know about quarterbacks is how quickly they can make decisions. When you draft them, they can have great Wonderlic tests, they can be 6'4", weigh 230 pounds, run, and have strong arms. But can they make split-second decisions with someone coming right down their face, and a guy flashes a color there, and they have to throw it down and low left? There's a lot they have to process in a short amount of time. You don't know that until they get in the heat of the battle.

There's so much to being a quarterback. It's not just the arm. That's why I (Moyer) would never draft a quarterback in the first round (unless it's John Elway, Peyton Manning, or some other once-in-a-generation, can't-miss quarterback).

Dave Krieg wasn't even drafted, and what a great story.

Krieg himself said, "Chuck got fed up with that [drafting quarterbacks who couldn't play]. He said, 'Look, I can take a guy like Dave Krieg and make him a winner.'

"Chuck was a work-ethic guy. Chuck was like, 'That's [quarterback is] not the main issue with this team.' Chuck knew, but the new owners had other plans, I guess. He liked the idea he had a quarterback like me. I practiced hard every play and didn't miss many practices. My attitude was: 'Don't leave your glove on the mound.'"

If you look at all the great quarterbacks, they're really good at something, and a lot of times it's not just football. That was the part I (Moyer) didn't see from Stouffer, McGwire, and Mirer. It wasn't that they didn't have athletic ability and strong arms. They did. That's why we drafted them. It was: are they competing every second of the day to be the very best they can be?

Maybe it's more of a compliment to the ones who make it. I've never met a great quarterback who wasn't incredibly competitive with a great work ethic. Those guys didn't have that.

chapter 6
Teammates

Jacob Green (79) and Fredd Young (50) take down the L.A. Raiders' Jay Schroeder in 1988 in Los Angeles.

Tez

To look at Cortez Kennedy, you would never think he could be such a dominant player. But he certainly was. So dominant that he went to a team-record eight Pro Bowls and was named the NFL Defensive Player of the Year in 1992.

It was the way he was built. He had such a low center of gravity. He was so quick with the first step and could turn his shoulders to get between people.

We ran a base 4-3, with our defensive tackles head up on the guards, but we would slant them right or left depending on the formation. You had a 50-50 chance of being right; and, although it wasn't rocket science, there was a way of being right every time: go the way Tez wants to go.

Tez loved to go left (which we called "Lenny"), so he would be down in his 3-point stance, and if I (Wyman) ever called out "Ricky, Ricky" (to go right), Tez would yell back, "Lenny, Lenny!" I would think about it for a second and then shout out, "Check…Lenny, Lenny!" We started calling him Lenny.

On the sideline, defensive coordinator Tom Catlin would ask me, "Why did you slant them to the left versus that formation?" I would reply, "Because that's the way Tez wanted to go." Tom would just nod in agreement. Who was going to argue with Tez?

Team photographer Corky Trewin took a great picture of the best hit I had in the NFL, and it was all due to Cortez. Tez was on a slant—to his left, of course—and although he couldn't make the play, he wiped out everything in front of me. When New York Giants fullback Jarrod Bunch cut back to the weak side, I was right there, unblocked, to make the hit.

I learned to sort of lurk just behind Cortez's back foot, and when he would take out two or sometimes three gaps on the strong side, the running back would cut to the backside, and that's when I would clean up. You might say I was one of those pilot fish that follow around the big sharks and feed off their scraps.

Those were the kind of things Cortez Kennedy would do for you.

In 1992 we designed blitzes knowing that he always got double-teamed. We didn't have to worry about teams' protection because wherever he was, that's where the protection went. We dictated by lining him up how they were going to protect, so we designed blitzes that way because we were 100 percent right. And we blitzed a lot because we had to.

In 1992 Tez had an astounding 14 sacks from the defensive tackle position, was second on the team with 92 tackles, and forced four fumbles. He was the best defender in the league that year.

But he never was remotely close to that dominant again. After that, I think double-teams got tiring for him. In 1994, if two guys hit him, he would be done. In 1992 those two and the fullback would take him on, and he kept coming.

Off the field, Tez was a very jovial guy and loved to laugh. One time there were about 12 of us sitting at a bar in Kirkland, and our union rep, James Jones, was holding court on the many virtues of the NFLPA. Cortez had questioned him on the amount of union dues we pay and the amount of money union president Gene Upshaw made.

Jones railed away at Tez, "What if you need representation...who you gonna call? What if there's a problem with your contract...who you gonna call? What about when your career is over and you need help adjusting to the real world...who you gonna call?"

Tez didn't miss a beat, quickly replying, "Shiiit... Ghostbusters!"

Cortez loved training camp and was always in a good mood, bouncing from room to room talking and laughing with everyone on the team. He didn't sleep much and, after bed check at 11:00, he could often be seen wandering the hallways.

One time I (Wyman) got up to go to the bathroom in the middle of the night. I left my door open and was doing my best to keep my eyes shut so I could get right back to sleep. I got back in

At his peak, Cortez Kennedy recorded an astounding 14 sacks from the defensive tackle position, was second on the team with 92 tackles, forced four fumbles, and was named NFL Defensive Player of the Year in 1992. Courtesy AP/Wide World Photos

my room, shut the door, and suddenly a very large figure emerged from my closet. He didn't yell, "Boo!" or anything like that because, well, he didn't have to. My heart jumped out of my chest, and I was left speechless. Tez took off down the hall laughing, and I lay there awake for another two hours. After that, I started taking my key to the bathroom so I could lock my door. How he fit in that closet, I'll never know.

Tez also was very generous, especially to the ball boys, equipment guys—everyone who had sort of thankless jobs. He took care of them. They all loved Cortez.

He would invite all of those guys, usually teenagers and guys in their early twenties, over to his house for barbecues and pool parties. He even let a few of them stay in his house during the off-season. The current head equipment guy, Eric Kennedy, was one of those kids who used to hang out over at Tez's place while he was attending Redmond High School.

Tez was very loyal to those who were loyal to him. One time he had an injury, and Dennis Erickson wanted him to play, anyway. The doctors stood up for Tez and told Dennis they would not let Kennedy play. So after that, every Monday or Tuesday, Tez would have a limousine pick up the doctors, and they would go to dinner because he appreciated that they were taking care of him and looking out for his best interests.

One thing I (Wyman) didn't like about Tez was that he was a slob. One year my locker was right next to his. His stuff was always spilling over into my locker, and finally at one point midway through the season, I had had enough. I came off the field and found his dirty jock strap lying on top of my clean street clothes.

I said, "Tez, you know I love you, but I can't live like this." I had Eric Kennedy move me to a nicer neighborhood, and they stuck a rookie next to Tez. Eventually, they left the locker next to him vacant.

It seemed only appropriate that he took up two lockers; after all, for most of his career, he took up at least two blockers.

Secondary Stories

(by Paul Moyer)

Million-Dollar Body, But No Confidence

Patrick Hunter was a tough one for the coaches. He was a great-looking athlete, built like a Greek god. He benched over 400 pounds. He could run and had decent change of direction. But he was never confident enough to make a play. He would be there, but he would hesitate. He was afraid to get beat deep. And you can't play this game scared.

He wasn't a bad player, but he was a guy who didn't make as many plays as he should have. But management knew cornerbacks were at a premium, and it never wanted to trade the former third-round pick.

Patrick would always ask, "We're not blitzing that much today, are we?" And I would just say, "Once you get out there, tell me if you are comfortable covering the guy." If he wasn't, we couldn't blitz because I didn't want a corner playing man to man when he wasn't confident.

Patrick was so nervous, and he didn't always get as much sleep as he should have the night before a game, so he would throw up before the game to the point where I'd ask, "Are you going to be able to play?" And he would say, "Yeah." Most of the time he was weak from lack of food, but he would use the No-Doz or the UpTime and find a way to play.

He had no body fat. But he used to drink that green stuff to make him get diarrhea because he wanted to make weight. So he was doing that, he was not eating much, and he'd say to me, "I can't go out and play; I'm just too sick." And I just looked at him and shook my head in disbelief.

Despite all of his woe-is-me theatrics, he was always in the lineup. He just wanted to hear us say how much we needed him. He needed that confidence boost.

Secondary Chance

Nesby Glasgow played five years with the Seahawks, but he almost didn't get signed because of a poor workout in 1988.

He was so distraught over getting cut by Indianapolis that he had a horrible workout with the Seahawks, and they didn't want to sign him. But he called the team back and said, "Look, I just wasn't into it. That wasn't my best. Let me come back and work out again." And when he came back and worked out again, they signed him.

To Nesby's credit, he was in great shape and certainly could still play. He played with us from 1988 to 1992 and started 30 games.

Former defensive back Nesby Glasgow, shown here in June 2002 as director of player programs for the Seahawks. Courtesy AP/Wide World Photos

The 11th Man

Who knew an 11th-round draft pick could be so valuable? But Dwayne Harper was.

We had a play called 88 Clamp, in which the nickel cornerback had to play man-to-man underneath coverage on the number-two receiver. And if he read an inside route by the outside receiver, he had to jump that route. Dwayne Harper was the only guy I've ever known who could do it.

When we lost him to free agency in 1994, I never called 88 Clamp again because I had run it for four or five years with him. He was so good at it.

Our defense went downhill when we lost him because he was so versatile and played so many positions. Losing him and Nate Odomes, who was injured before he ever played for us in 1994, killed us.

All of a sudden we had undrafted free agent Orlando Watters starting, and he was too slow and too short for us to depend on as a starter.

We lost in overtime against Cincinnati in 1994 because Watters was covering some guy from Cincinnati who was 6′4″. They threw a jump ball about 50 yards. Watters was in perfect position; he just couldn't get high enough to make the play.

I Got Lucky

Eddie Anderson was a sixth-round draft pick in 1986. He was an incredible specimen. He ran a 4.4-second 40-yard dash, was 215 pounds, benched-pressed around 500 pounds. I remember thinking, "I'm gone."

Then we got out on the football field, and I thought, "No way." I could play every position, and he didn't know where to go out there.

When he hit you, he killed you. But he had to find you first. We let him go because Ralph Hawkins ran a very complicated third-down package. We had a very smart secondary, led by Kenny Easley and Dave Brown, but Eddie didn't fit in.

To Eddie's credit, he went to the Raiders and became a very productive safety.

Sometimes It Is about the Race

In 1991 Rod Perry, Joe Vitt, and myself disagreed with Chuck Knox over which of two cornerbacks to keep on the team heading into the season. (No one ever argued with Chuck; we did sometimes disagree, however.)

Malcolm Frank was an undrafted rookie from Baylor that year. Brian Davis was one of the few white corners in the league and a fourth-year guy we had picked up from Washington's Super Bowl team.

Malcolm had quick feet and was a better player in practice than Brian. And Chuck said, "I don't care. We traded for Brian. He can run, he's big [6′2″], and you've got to have those kinds of guys. Malcolm looks good in practice. If you put him out there, every once in a while he'll shine. But at the end of the day, he's a guy who just can't play in this league."

Rod, Joe, and myself argued that Malcolm was a better player than Brian Davis. Brian was fast, but he wasn't a great cover guy and wasn't a physical player. We just didn't like him as much as we liked Malcolm.

Toward the end of camp, Chuck called over Brian Davis and Malcolm Frank and said, "I want you guys to come over here. You guys are going to race."

Brian Davis obviously sensed that something was up because he asked, "Am I racing to make the team?"

Chuck said, "I just want to see something on this."

Brian was clearly faster than Malcolm, but Chuck wanted to prove his point that Brian was much faster.

We knew Chuck was going to win this battle, and the three of us sarcastically said among ourselves, "Well, if we lined up in a three-point stance and the DBs always ran forward, then Brian's the guy. But last we checked, we've got to backpedal, stop, and change direction."

So Chuck had them race, Brian won and made the team, and we cut Malcolm.

We opened with New Orleans, and Brian picked off a pass and returned it for a touchdown. And Chuck walked up to us and said, "I told you so. This guy's a good player. Enough said."

The funny thing was that Brian hated Chuck after that race. He complained about having to race to win a job, and here Chuck was on his side the whole time.

The next year, when Chuck was gone, we kept both Brian and Malcolm. But if Malcolm would have run a little faster in 1991, he would have made the team then.

Safety Switch

In the 1994 draft, we were looking to trade Robert Blackmon for a safety out of Nebraska named Toby Wright. Rusty Tillman really wanted him because he was a thumper, and Rusty didn't like the way Blackmon played. But Blackmon didn't make a lot of mistakes and was a decent cover guy; he just didn't make a lot of plays and wasn't a knockout tackler.

The Rams had just picked Wright in the second round, and Rusty wanted me to convince Tom Flores to trade for him. But I wasn't sure. I knew what I had in Robert and didn't really want to take a rookie and start him.

I talked it through for a minute or so, listing the pros and cons. And Flores, who usually never raised his voice, said loudly and sternly, "I don't want to hear you talk this through. Do you want to make the trade or not?"

And sheepishly I said, "Yeah, let's make the trade." Flores walked out of the room, and Rusty looked at me, shook his head, and said, "I don't even know if I believed you."

And I said, "I don't know if I believed myself."

Lucky for us, the Rams didn't want to make the trade, so Blackmon continued a pretty productive career for us, and Toby Wright was never heard from.

Jacob, Joe, and Jeff

Jacob Green, Jeff Bryant, and Joe Nash—our starting defensive linemen in the 1980s—were the tightest three guys on the team for the longest time.

They were good players, too. Jacob was the most gifted of the three. He was a very good pass rusher who holds the team record with 116 sacks. If he had been in a 4–3 defense, he probably would have had even more sacks. He had such a great first step.

Jeff "Boogie" Bryant was a hard-nosed, get-it-done guy. Everybody loved him. He almost never got mad, but when he did, you knew you were in trouble.

Joe had the greatest swim move; that's why he had so many blocked PATs and field goals. He owns the team records with 10 blocked extra-point kicks and eight blocked field goals.

We were playing the Chargers in 1989. With less than a minute left, we were up 17–16, and they were on their 4-yard line.

Jim McMahon was quarterbacking, and we were playing a two-deep zone. McMahon went deep to Anthony Miller, and on a play that I (Moyer) normally would make, I didn't get there. Miller caught it in stride, but he tripped and fell around the 40-yard line. I managed to dive and tag him down. But I was thinking, "Oh, my God, I lost the game for us." I was in position, read it right, and they still beat me. (That was when I knew I was done. And 1989 was, in fact, my final year as a player.)

The Chargers lined up for a field goal that would win it, and I went to Joe Nash and gave him my greatest Knute Rockne impersonation. "Come on, Joe! You've got to block this kick! You've got to block it!"

And sure enough, Joe blocked it, and we won 17–16.

To this day, Joe tells me, "You got me so fired up."

He blocked that and won the game for us.

From my (Wyman's) perspective as a linebacker, you loved playing behind Joe because, if he couldn't make the play, he was going to allow you to make it by grabbing a guard so he couldn't get upfield and block you.

In 1990 Joe played hurt that whole year. After the season, he needed surgeries on his ankle and elbow, and he had played the last game with kidney stones. He had ignored all of that stuff the whole season, so he decided to get it all fixed at once. I saw him in the locker room two days after the last game, and one arm was in a sling, the other held a cane, and they had fixed him up with a catheter for the kidney stones. He was the poster child for misery.

During that Monday night game in 1987, Bo Jackson busted off a 90-yard touchdown run against us. On that play, Jeff Bryant was playing left end in our 3–4 defense and I (Moyer) was playing left linebacker because they had pulled the linebackers out and put the faster defensive backs in.

Bo broke it down our right side. Boogie was in my way among a crowd of linemen there, and I pushed Jeff down, trying to scrape through to get over there. But there was no way. We were 10 yards away, and Bo Jackson was speeding down the sideline.

Boogie never got mad at anybody, but he got up after I had tripped him and was so upset with me, yelling, "I cannot believe you pushed me from behind!"

And I said to him, "I pushed you from behind, but were you going to get him? Did you really think you were going to catch Bo Jackson? I don't know about that, Boogie."

He literally thought the reason Bo scored is because I pushed him down.

The linebackers used to joke about Jake, Joe, and Jeff, calling them "the mafia." You learned early on that whether a play was their fault or your fault, *it was always your fault*. Those guys stuck together, and it's what made them such a great unit for so many years.

Freelancin' Freddie

Fredd Young was a mini–Lawrence Taylor. He was so athletic and naturally strong.

From the time Fredd came to us as a third-round draft pick in 1984, he made dynamic plays. He was a great punt-blocker. He would get through the line so fast, he would be able to grab the punter's foot as he was dropping the ball. That's how he went to the Pro Bowl his first two years—because he was so good on special teams.

And then he became a Pro Bowl linebacker the next two years. He just had a knack for making plays, kind of like Lawrence Taylor. His first year as a starter, in 1985, he led the team with 118 tackles. In 1986 he had 121 tackles and six sacks. And in 1987 he had nine sacks and five forced fumbles.

But a lot of his plays came on unplanned blitzes. One year half his sacks came when he was supposed to be in a zone drop. He was supposed to drop into coverage, but Young would go after the quarterback.

Keith Butler usually would have to cover for him when he did that.

"You kind of had to play off him a bit and get him lined up a bit," Butler said. "In our defense, you had to be disciplined. Sometimes, he would just take off and go rush the quarterback while he was supposed to be in a zone coverage. I asked him one time, 'Freddie, what the heck are you doing?' He said, 'I thought I could get there.'

"He was a great athlete and could make plays. But he did stuff that would totally screw up the defense. It was frustrating for Tom Catlin, and sometimes it was frustrating for me."

When a guy like Fredd starts making more mistakes than plays, you have to get rid of him. And that's what happened when the Seahawks traded him to Indianapolis in 1988. They said, "He's not making enough plays to warrant his freelancing."

We got two first-round draft picks for him, and one of them turned into Cortez Kennedy, so that was a pretty good deal.

Soft Body, Softer Hands

John L. Williams did not look like an NFL player. He had a soft body, didn't lift weights, didn't have great speed. Mack Strong's a rock. But John L. was more like Jell-O.

His nickname was "Chumley," like the walrus with the rounded shoulders and long arms in the Tennessee Tuxedo cartoons. Off the field, he moved very slowly and sort of shuffled around very quietly.

One time during camp we had a night off, so Dave Krieg took John L. and me (Wyman) out on his boat to fish on Lake Sammamish. John L. sat there with his line in the water the whole time, not saying a word while Dave and I argued about everything from cover-2 to farm subsidies. The only thing John L. said the whole time was, "You two are gonna scare the fish away."

In the off-season, he would go back to Florida and kill alligators and stuff. Once camp started, he would walk right off the bass boat and onto the field, and you could tell he hadn't done a damn thing to get ready for football. But he was such a natural that he would be up to speed two practices later.

He had the softest hands, and that's why he caught everything so easily.

I have a picture of me hugging him out on the field after we beat the Raiders to win the AFC West in 1988. He won the game for us with a 75-yard touchdown on a screen pass.

He was an all-around great player. I just remember those hands.

Fenner's Rep

Running back Derrick Fenner had a reputation from the time he spent in jail just before the Seahawks drafted him in 1989.

He never was tried on any charge and was released after 44 days, which is what prompted him to wear No. 44 with the Seahawks.

He was actually a very nice, normal guy, but he really liked playing up that thug role. He was like the Fonz—he liked to intimidate people using his notoriety. And most guys steered clear of him.

Then one day a lineman named Curt Singer shattered that image. Singer was a red-headed country boy from West Virginia and was built like a big block, probably 6'5" and 290 pounds. It was quite a contrast in body types, because Fenner was chiseled like a statue at 6'3" and 225 pounds.

They got into a heated verbal exchange in the locker room one day, and Fenner approached Singer in a threatening way. But the hulking tackle had no reason to be scared of the smaller running back and didn't even blink an eye. He just grabbed his helmet off the hook in his locker and—wham!—slammed Fenner over the head with it. Simple and effective. Fenner ended up with stitches and didn't mess with anybody after that.

Not surprisingly, Fenner was only a Seahawk for three years. He had one pretty good year, rushing for 859 yards and 14 touchdowns as our starting back in 1990, and then he bounced to Cincinnati (1992–1994) and Oakland (1995–1997).

On a long flight home once, Derrick told me (Wyman) about his background and how tough he had it growing up on the streets and around gangs.

I told him he was blessed with a tremendous amount of athletic talent, and I said, "It's all about the choices you make from here on out."

He obviously made some good ones because he lasted nine years in the NFL and then became a successful businessman and wonderful family man.

Gaines-ville and Butts

You wouldn't necessarily classify Greg Gaines as a cerebral player, but he certainly wasn't dumb—he just sounded that way. Keith Butler was from the South, too, and he *was* a cerebral player—but again, everything was "dad gum" this and "ya'll" that. Being a West Coast guy, I used to like to criticize their accents and tell them they were a couple of hillbillies.

Although they were best of friends, they loved to argue. I called them the Hatfields and McCoys. One time I was sitting there watching them playfully argue back and forth in their Southern twang, and suddenly I started hearing the banjo playing in my head (think *Deliverance*), "Da Na Neer-Neer Neer-Neer Neer-Neer Neeeer. Da Na Neer-Neer Neer-Neer Neer-Neer Neeeer." I think that song was called "Dueling Banjos." Well, this version was "Dueling Hillbillies."

Butler recounted a story about him and Gaines from 1983, when the Seahawks upset the Dolphins in a playoff game in Miami:

"Greg Gaines was a nut. He was my roommate on the road.…We got down there so late, we were in bed around 2:30 AM Saturday. We had a meeting at 11:00 AM and had set up a wake-up call for 10:30.

"The phone rang, but Gaines just went back to sleep. Next thing I know, the phone rang again. We looked at the clock, and it was 11:15. We both jumped out of bed, and Gaines was telling me not to answer it. Well, I answered, and it was Tom Catlin. He asked if we had gotten a wake-up call, and I said yes. Then he told us to get down to the meeting. Gaines was so mad because he had wanted me to tell Catlin that we hadn't gotten a wake-up call so we wouldn't get in trouble.

"Chuck Knox happened to be sitting on our bus (we had one for the offense and one for the defense) on the way to the game. He rarely said much on those bus rides, but he asked us if we had gotten a wake-up call that morning. And I told him we had.

"Gaines just went crazy. He kept saying, 'You idiot, we're going to get cut after this game. We're going to get cut.' He was so afraid Chuck was going to cut us for sleeping in.

"Well, we won the game, and I think Chuck was too happy to think about it because we didn't get cut."

I (Wyman) learned so much football from Keith Butler my rookie year. He used to call me "boy" and still does every time I call him.

When I first met him, he came up to me in the weight room and said, "Boy, you were drafted to replace me. I know that. So you might as well start learning the game. I want you to sit by me in film and stand by me out at practice."

I was shocked. I knew I had been drafted to replace him, too, but I thought he would hate me for it. The one year I spent with him as a teammate, I learned more football than the previous eight years put together.

Butler and Gaines used to call people "idiots," and in their twang, it would come out "idjit."

One time the Seahawks were in Washington, D.C., looking at national monuments and various historical places and artifacts. Gaines turned to Butler, who was acting as his tour guide, and said, "Man, I don't know any of this stuff."

Gaines thought about it for a minute and then said, "That's okay, Vitt's an idjit, too." Poor Joe Vitt—how did he get dragged into this?

Gaines was one of the toughest players of all time. He once split his hand wide open in a game against the Redskins in

Washington. The doctors told him they needed to take him to the hospital, but he said, "No, I'm not leaving." So they stapled his hand and wrapped it up, and he kept playing.

He was the toughest guy. Bullethead led with his head every time. How many times would he be fined in today's world? He couldn't play. He led with his head every time, and he always had blood trickling from his forehead in every game.

He was kind of scary. He always had a real psychotic look in his eye, and it was well known that you just do not mess with Gaines.

If you watch that clip of Bo Jackson running over Brian Bosworth in that Monday night game in 1987, Gaines comes in late and swings his arm like he is trying to punch him. Every time he tackled somebody he was trying to inflict as much pain as possible. He would punch and flail his arms and drive guys into the turf—anything he could get away with…and some he couldn't. Once we combined on a tackle of Ickey Woods in Cincinnati, and I remember hearing him scream, "I'm going to f*cking kill you!" He was just a nasty, scary dude.

Before my first game in the pros, I (Wyman) was nervously pacing the locker room, and I wandered into the showers. The lights were low, but I could make out Gaines standing there in full pads, smoking a cigarette. He looked at me with that crazy look of his, took a long drag off his cigarette and said, "Ya'll ready to go?"

He was a great guy, but he was the meanest player I (Moyer) ever played with. He was game-day mean. He was just a fighter. He didn't care. Some guys have that mentality that they love to fight, and he was a fighter.

Rufe, Rufe, Rufe!

Rufus Porter was a guy who was on the bubble (almost cut) his rookie year in 1988. He made the team because of his special-teams play.

The speedy Rufus Porter went from being almost cut to a defensive force for the Seahawks after being drafted in 1988.

Special-teams coach Rusty Tillman used to time guys in a flying 40-yard dash. You would get a 10-yard head start, and then he would time you for 40 yards in order to simulate running down on a kickoff. Rufus recorded the fastest "flying 40" on the team. During the preseason in 1988, Norm Johnson hit a kickoff that was fielded on the goal line, and Rufus made the tackle on the 7-yard line. He almost outran the ball. That's how he made the team.

Rufus quickly developed into one of our best pass rushers, and he was one of the main guys who brought in the no-flinch rule because he would always try to get offensive linemen to false start. When Ray Roberts was a rookie in 1992, Porter was lined up across from him in practice, and the first thing Rufus did was say, "Boo!" He did that all the time in games, trying to get guys to move. Then he'd get them thinking about it, and when he came around the corner at full speed, he would be almost parallel to the ground.

He liked to come across as an "aw, shucks" country boy, but Rufus was pretty smart. And a great guy, too.

He was the nicest, quietest guy in the world, but he would back down from nobody on the field. That was obvious in a 1990 Monday night game when he and Boomer Esiason went at it.

It started when Rufus slammed Esiason to the turf on a play that had been blown dead. Rufus didn't hear the whistle because it was so loud in the Kingdome. Esiason and Rufus started pushing each other, and Rufus actually swung at Boomer and got a penalty. And that just fired up Rufus even more.

On the next play, he batted down one of Esiason's passes and taunted Esiason by pointing in his face. That fired up the fans, who started chanting, "Rufe, Rufe, Rufe." They were so loud that the Bengals committed a delay of game. Then, with the crowd as loud as ever, Porter knocked down another pass by Esiason.

Rufus was a man possessed in that game, and we ended up upsetting the Bengals 31–16.

As Joe Nash said, "Rufus would not step down from anybody. He was not a big guy and wasn't real intense. But once he got going, he was hard to stop."

Blades Runner

I (Wyman) loved Brian Blades. He came in as a second-round pick in 1988 and contributed right away. He was tough, and the one thing I appreciate more in a teammate than anything else is toughness. And I don't mean just physically. He was mentally and emotionally tough, too. He didn't let anything get him down. As Chuck Knox would say, "He was never too high and he was never too low."

Brian was a gamer. He was small and didn't have great speed, but he was a good route runner and was sneaky fast.

He came from the University of Miami, where they had a thug reputation, but Brian was anything but a thug. He was liked by everyone on the team and was one of those players who had friends on both sides of the ball. He was a very happy and likable guy.

When his cousin was tragically shot and killed while trying to take a gun from Brian in July 1995, it changed Brian's personality. He went from fun-loving, easygoing, and happy to depressed. He never was the same after that—on or off the field. While he played well in 1995, after that it seemed like he didn't want to play anymore. It took an emotional toll on him, which hurt him as much as any physical ailments did in his final three years.

Paul Skansi: The Human Target

We used to call Paul Skansi "the Human Target." He would go across the middle and make the tough catches that no one else wanted to make. He would invariably get blasted every time, but he always held on to the ball.

Dave Krieg remembered that, too: "He would just take a beating, catch third-down passes. He was a very clutch receiver. You could always depend on him. He gave you everything he had. He epitomized what the Seahawks were all about. He got the most out of his ability that a guy could get."

The tough but likable Brian Blades reels in a catch against the Arizona Cardinals in October 1995.

Bad Citizen Kane

Tommy Kane played receiver for us from 1988 to 1992. He was kind of a cool, laid-back dude who was a little on the rough side. He was always clowning around in the locker room, and he never let anybody see his sensitive side. But he showed it to me once in a conversation we (Kane and Wyman) had.

He had gone to Walla Walla Penitentiary to meet with some of the prisoners, including some in isolation, and when he came back, Tommy said to me, "Some of those guys aren't allowed to touch anyone. Can you imagine what it would be like to never touch anyone?" He went on and on about it—it was a strangely sensitive moment for him.

It also turned out to be an odd kind of foreshadowing because in 2004 Kane pleaded guilty to manslaughter in the stabbing death of his wife and was sentenced to 18 years in prison.

Lifesaving Missed Tackle

I (Moyer) tell Paul Johns I saved his life.

In 1984 he was tackled on a punt return and temporarily paralyzed. They found out he had stenosis, a narrowing of the spine, in his neck. It was a degenerative condition that you don't learn about until something like that happens.

The guy who tackled him on the punt return was my guy. So I tell Paul, "I saved your life. The one time I missed a block in all of my years on the punt-return team, I saved your life."

"Do I Hypnotize You with My Eyes?"

Bobby Joe Edmonds became our kick returner after the team drafted him in the fifth round in 1986. He wasn't a great athlete or that hard to tackle. He wouldn't run away from anybody. But he had a burst of speed and had what makes a return man so good—the start-stop moves.

He was very good at setting up the blocks. And there was a point where we felt we could break it all the time.

Off the field, he had a strut about him, and Jeff Bryant and some other guys followed him around and thought he was cool.

He would stay out late a lot because he didn't really have to practice being the kick returner. So he had a lot of blood-shot eyes; he would wear sunglasses in the meetings because he was "B.J.E."

Jeff would talk about him like he was so cool, and I (Wyman) would tell Jeff, "Boogie, you're a starter, you're a former first-round pick, you're older than him. What are you doing following him around?"

But Bobby Joe was confident and had that effect on some people.

He had funky-colored eyes, and he would approach women at bars and ask, "Do I hypnotize you with my eyes?"

He would strike out eight times out of 10, but those two made it all worth it for him.

Bevo Did What It Took

Bryan Millard always started strong—literally—but he usually couldn't finish that way.

Every off-season, he would work hard to build his body up. He would turn himself into a 285-pound guy in a 240-pound body. And he would play like a Pro Bowler early in the year. But by the end of the season, after his size went away and he was probably down to 270, he just wasn't the same player as he had been at the beginning.

He was the kind of guy who would do whatever it took to win. He was a battler. He used to get manhandled by bigger guys, but he would fight and scratch and do the best he could. And that's what made him one of our better linemen in the 1980s.

Fightin' Feasel

My (Wyman's) first roommate with the Seahawks was center Grant Feasel, who had just been signed from the Minnesota Vikings. Grant was married and had two children at the time and was the nicest guy in the world. That's why it was so surprising to me how he behaved on the field. He would transform himself into a different person. Not that I was a model citizen out there, but Grant was so squeaky clean. He never cursed, and I would listen to him tell his wife he loved her over the phone and sing lullabies to his children.

But once he stepped on the field, he would do whatever it took to get the job done. In practice, Grant and I would always go at it;

we probably got into a full-blown fistfight at least four times a week. But once practice ended, all was forgotten and forgiven.

We were like that old Looney Toons cartoon where the coyote and the sheep dog would punch into the time clock, beat the hell out of each other all day, and then punch out. "Good night, Sam." "Good night, Ralph."

"If You're Scared, Say You're Scared"

Ron Essink started 70 games from 1980 to 1985, but when he was done, it was obvious. Before a game against the Raiders in 1985, Ron Essink didn't want to play, and we didn't know why—other than the obvious fact that he would be going up against Lyle Alzado and Howie Long and those guys.

I think he played, but none of the players felt they could count on him. You can't go into a game saying, I don't want to play. Needless to say, Ron wasn't with us after that season.

Meanwhile, Kenny Easley huddled up all of the defensive backs before that Raiders game and said, "This game ain't for the faint of heart. If you're scared, say you're scared!" And he walked through the locker room, repeatedly telling people, "If you're scared, say you're scared!"

That one stuck for a long time: "If you're scared, say you're scared!"

Nervous? Or Just a BSer?

Who would get the most nervous?

Every game, within the first series, Reggie McKenzie would get so nervous that he would throw up—right through his face mask, on the sideline, in the huddle. Every game. It was just a matter of us waiting for it.

McKenzie started a thing where he would hold up his index finger in the "number-one" sign. But it didn't mean you were number one. It meant you were the number-one bullshitter of all time—you tell more bullshit than anybody.

Reggie started it, and Jacob Green ran with it. Curt Warner and I (Moyer) didn't take crap from anybody, and Reggie and Jacob would always say, "You guys are the One of All Time."

We'd always say Jacob was, and we've kept that one going through the years.

We got him really good before a playoff game against the Washington Redskins in 2005. We had our radio show set up outside the stadium, and there were about 2,000 fans milling about before the game.

We brought some of the Ring of Honor guys on our radio show, and I introduced Jacob to the fans: "You all know this guy from the past. He was a great player for the Seahawks, so I want everybody to raise a finger and help me welcome Jacob Green, the One of All Time."

As 2,000 people raised a finger, Jacob walked out with a big grin, acknowledging that I had nailed him at his own game quite publicly.

chapter 7
Tough Guys

Paul Moyer grabs hold and won't let go of Charles White of the Los Angeles Rams in an October 1988 game.

Moyer's Manhood

Injuries and playing hurt are part of the NFL. Playing a tough, physical, bruising game like this, you're always going to get hurt. But there is a difference between being hurt and being injured. If you have a dislocated finger or a bruised shoulder, you're hurt. Get out there and play. If you have a broken foot or torn knee ligament, you're injured. You're not going to play.

So here's a story about a guy who thought he was hurt—and found out much later that he was actually injured.

Injuries played a big part during the 1986 season. We started 5-2, but the injury bug hit us, and we went on a four-game losing streak.

After we lost to Cincinnati in the final game of the streak, the team put Kenny Easley on injured reserve because of turf toe that had bothered him all season. I (Moyer) replaced him in the lineup, and somehow we managed to win the next four games to put ourselves in position to make the playoffs.

We had to beat Denver in the last game of the year to have a chance at the playoffs.

There was about a minute and a half left in the first half. The Broncos had a guy named Orson Mobley—a big tight end with knees about the size of both my legs. They had been running these little hitch routes, and I was jumping all over the route. I could tell John Elway was getting kind of frustrated, so they decided to run a hook-and-go, and as I turned to run with Orson, he grabbed me, pulled me toward him, and kneed me in the groin. I went down hard and fast.

The trainers came out, and they thought I had blue balls, where your testicle is up inside you. So they told me, "We're going to have you jump up and down on the bench and try to release it." So I was jumping up and down, and I got to the point where I was so nauseated that I was dry-heaving on the side.

With about 30 seconds left in the half, the guy who went in for me got beat for a touchdown. So as I was walking to the locker room, I was thinking, "I've gotta play."

Defensive backs wanted to be as light as possible so they could be as fast as they could, so we didn't wear very much protection—no thigh pads, knee pads, or cups. But when we went into the locker room, they put a soft cup and a hard cup on me to protect it because clearly something was not right there.

After getting off the training table very delicately, I went out and played the second half. But I was bent over after every play, cramping up. People asked me later, "How'd you play?" And I said, "That's what adrenaline does." But in between it was the worst pain I had ever felt.

After we won the game, I gingerly walked into the locker room and carefully pulled down my pants—and everybody groaned and gasped in shock at what it looked like. I had a ruptured testicle and was black and blue. I had so much blood, my testicle was almost down to my knee. Well, not that far. But it was hanging a lot lower than it should have been. Think of a water balloon when it has too much water and just stretches toward the ground. That's what it looked like.

Luckily, there just happened to be a urologist there, and he looked at it and said, "Oh, that's not good. We need to get you to the hospital."

So they put me in an ambulance, and I went in to have surgery.

Now as luck would have it, *Parade* magazine had recently done a feature on the 10 most eligible bachelors in the NFL. The Seahawks had nominated me (why? I have no idea), and I had done this whole photo spread for the magazine.

So the day after this game and the surgery, I opened the paper, and the headline read, "Moyer Plays with Ruptured Testicle."

Now, when you're single, that's not something you want getting out there.

But this does have a happy ending. I ended up marrying a beautiful woman who happened to be a SeaGal, and my wife still loves me, and we have two beautiful children.

I got a job out of it, too. Chuck Knox said, "Anybody who plays with a ruptured testicle is my kind of guy." And I swear that's why he hired me to be an assistant coach after I retired in 1989.

Of course, if I had known the testicle was ruptured, I might have thought twice about going back into the game. Because it turns out I was not just hurt; I was, in fact, injured.

Heck of an Uppercut

When tackle Andy Heck was drafted in the first round in 1989, he was seen as kind of a tough guy—until he went up against Marcus Cotton one day. Marcus was an outside linebacker from USC we had acquired from the Atlanta Falcons. He wasn't very big, but he could bench-press close to 500 pounds and was extremely powerful.

I didn't know how good of a fighter he was until we were doing a pass-rush drill in training camp and he beat Andy a couple of times. Andy got frustrated and hit him. While Andy was slugging away at him, Marcus grabbed Heck's face mask took one step backward and hit Andy with two vicious uppercuts to the chin. It dropped Andy right to his knees.

The whole thing was on film, so that night, in lieu of our normal meetings, Rusty Tillman told all of us linebackers, "We're just going to do one thing tonight. I'm going to show you how to fight on the football field."

So we watched that film in slow motion for about 20 minutes, and that was our meeting. Rusty evaluated the fight like he was "the Fight Doctor" Ferdie Pacheco, saying things like, "Watch what he does here," and, "Oh, look at Andy's knees—he just crumpled him."

A Ballsy Strategy

Rusty would always say, "It's not a sin to be held, but it's a sin to stay held. And if someone's holding you, which is illegal, you can't wait for the official to throw a flag. You have to take care of it yourself."

Rusty also used to say, "I don't care if you have to kick a guy in the balls. Take care of it!" He would throw out an oft-used Knoxism, "That guy has his hand in your back pocket!"

Most guys didn't take that solution literally, but linebacker Joe Cain did. Joe was running down on a punt against the San Diego Chargers, and a guy was holding him the whole way down, so Joe stopped, gathered himself, and kicked the guy right in the balls. To this day, it was the funniest thing I've ever seen on film. And even funnier than that was the next play: Joe did it again, and the guy kicked him right back. It went back and forth. These two players were stopped in the middle of the field having a nut-kicking contest.

Joe continued to do it, and after a while players around the league became aware of it. Joe told me that he did it to this tough little linebacker in Pittsburgh named Jerry Olsavsky. Joe gave him his best shot, and Jerry O just stood there and said, "Hey, that shit don't work on me." Joe told me this and laughingly said, "That's one bad dude." We started calling him "Iron Balls" Olsavsky!

The Best Fight I Ever Saw

Bryan Millard and Jacob Green were in the best fight I (Wyman) ever saw.

There was a lot of animosity between them. Bryan, our starting right guard, had really cheap-shotted defensive lineman Roy Hart in practice one time. Chuck Knox was pretty outraged by it, so he made Bryan get up and apologize to Roy in front of the entire team. The apology was less than sincere, and Jacob and the rest of the D-linemen weren't having it. Those guys stuck together.

All during training camp, the rivalry between Jacob and Bryan continued to build. It finally erupted during a team period one afternoon, and Rusty Tillman and I had front-row seats. It was like watching these two big behemoths go at it. They locked up, and it looked like Bevo (Millard) had Green, when all of a sudden Jake bent his body to one side and violently slammed Bevo to the

Jacob Green's body slam of a teammate during a training-camp practice led his teammates to respect him as much as his opponents.

ground. Millard came down hard right at our feet, and it shook the ground.

Defensive line coach George Dyer ran over there, yelling in his high-pitched voice: "Jake, your hands! Your hands!" He didn't want Jake to break his hands.

Jake definitely got the best of Bryan, and after the whole thing was broken up, Rusty and I looked at each other wide-eyed and at the same time said, "That was awesome!"

The thing about those fights is, as a spectator, there's nothing you can do. The only thing you can do is get hurt. They're like two bears. Two 300-pounders going at it. What are you going to do?

One time Greg Gaines and an offensive lineman went at it, and Tom Catlin tried to jump in and break it up. He came out of the pile with a big, fat, swollen lip!

How Catlin Handled Chaos

Catlin was used to delivering that kind of damage.

It's always the quiet ones you should fear, and that was the case with Tom. He was a tough, old bird—a fan in L.A. found that out the hard way. Tom was a two-time All-American linebacker at the University of Oklahoma and played for the Cleveland Browns and Philadelphia Eagles for five seasons.

After the Seahawks lost the AFC Championship Game at the Coliseum in January 1984, the fans stormed the field, and the celebration turned into a riot. Police were called, an emergency helicopter landed on the field to aid someone who had been stabbed…it was pandemonium. We tried to get out of there as quickly as we could.

As Tom walked off the field next to linebacker Sam Merriman, a Raiders fan came running up to Tom and pointed his finger right in Tom's face. In one fluid motion, Tom grabbed the guy by the throat, slammed him up against a wall, and blasted him in the face with his fist. After the players broke it up, Tom turned to Sam and, in his typical, dry, understated fashion, said, "You didn't see that, okay?"

Toe Shots

In 1987 Kenny Easley had the kidney problem, which no one knew about at the time. But he also had turf toe. Kenny was a tough guy, but those shots were not fun.

I (Moyer) remember one time he held my hand as they shot up his toe for the 10th game in a row so he could play. He said, "Paul, the shot is unbearable."

For as strong as he was, it was weird how Kenny wanted people around him in times of crisis. But then he would turn back into a warrior, put his helmet on, and strut out to the field like nothing was wrong. The thing I admired about him the most was he played at a high level with turf toe and a kidney problem and never complained.

Linebacker Bruce Scholtz had the same deal. He had turf toe from week eight on. I (Wyman) can't imagine the distraction that would be to know you have to have a big needle stuck in your toe before every game and at halftime.

I remember walking by one time when the doctor was shooting up Bruce's toe, and I couldn't believe how barbaric it was. Once the needle goes into the joint, they have to move it around to make sure the novocaine gets to the right spot. There was blood everywhere. The only thing Scholtz could do to handle the pain was bite down hard on a towel.

chapter 8
Assistants

Chuck Knox, shown here during a November 1988 game, was old-school through and through.

TomCat

Tom Catlin was the best coach I (Wyman) ever had. He was an incredible teacher and such a calm football mind, especially on game day.

He had the perfect demeanor to be a defensive coordinator in the NFL. He was unflappable; you could not rattle him.

You could rattle me, however, just as New York Giants center Bart Oates did one game. It was 1992, so of course we were losing. The frustration of a fifth straight loss, coupled with the fact that the umpire refused to call holding on Oates the entire game, finally got the best of me. So I did something we used to call "taking a play off," which is when you forget about the ball for a play and go exact street justice on someone. I grabbed Oates by the jersey and pulled him toward me while backpedaling as fast as I could. When I got him off-balance enough, I rabbit-punched him in the back of the head. I hit him so hard his head practically bounced off the turf, and when he got up, a fight ensued.

I came off the field after that play, and Tom, who apparently hadn't seen the fight, walked over to ask me what was happening out there in the running game. I didn't tell him I didn't know because I was too busy getting revenge. I was hyperventilating and still in a rage, and between gasps I said in a high-pitched tone, "I'm too pissed to talk right now." He turned his eyes from me back to his clipboard and said very calmly, "Okay, let me know when you can."

Without Question, Catlin Was a Great Coach

In his meetings, when he put in a defensive game plan each week, he would say in his monotone drone, "Please hold your questions until the end."

Ninety-nine times out of 100, by the time he was done, there would be no questions. I remember one time he put a defense in, and at the end I asked him something, and he said, "That's a good question." I was so proud of myself. I finally cracked Tom Catlin!

When he came to Seattle in 1983, he knew that he knew more about defense than Chuck Knox. Chuck had certain things that he didn't want to run because they were unsound. He said, "If that's unsound, you cannot run it. I don't want you guys to bump-and-run because of the four things that can happen, three of them are bad." He hated bump-and-run coverage and wouldn't let Tom Catlin do it.

But as soon as Chuck Knox left, Tom incorporated bump-and-run because he and Tom Flores believed it enhanced the defense.

Catlin became the best coach I (Moyer) have ever worked with or played under.

He was such a great listener. He was secure enough to take information people would offer and learn something, or to say, "I don't know that," or, "That's a good idea, but here's how we're going to run it."

With a lot of coaches, they get really insecure, and they don't want you to question or challenge them. With Tom, if it was a good question, he really would think about it. He used to call me the "what-if" coach because I would ask, "What if...?"

He would pull me aside and say, "Paul, what do you want to run? And why?" And he would listen. That's the sign of a good coach.

All of Catlin's players felt that way about him.

Keith Butler, who played five of his 10 seasons for Catlin, said, "Tom Catlin was such a good coach. He was so detail-oriented and did a great job of preparing us and a great job of listening to his players. He was the type of guy who felt like he didn't have all of the answers, and that humility made him a great coach."

Joe Nash, who played nose tackle for us, said Catlin was ahead of his time: "We were so well prepared when he was coaching us. It was almost like he knew what their game plan was. I remember playing the Chargers down in San Diego on Monday night, and I was covering Chuck Muncie out of the backfield. We were playing a zone blitz long before it was popular."

Before we played the Detroit Lions and Barry Sanders in 1990, Tom had come up with a plan to slow down Barry. He never used the word "stop"—just "slow down." His plan was simple: stay home! That means if your responsibility is the weakside A gap, stay in that gap, and do not give in to the temptation to chase after Barry no matter where he goes.

On one play, Barry ran a sweep to the outside. My (Wyman's) responsibility was the weakside A gap. Barry was all the way in the strongside D gap, which was four gaps and 15 yards away from me.

There was an epic struggle playing out in my head. Tom's voice was saying: "Stay home!" But I was thinking, "This is crazy. He's gonna get away!…Hey, wait. He's coming back!…Here he is! Holy shit! Tom was right!"

That was the first time I (Moyer) had ever heard a coach say, "Do not try to tackle this guy."

"Do not tackle this guy. Just grab him," Tom said, because Barry was so small, you could grab him by the jersey and pull him to the ground; but if you tried to tackle him, he would make you miss.

We did a good job on him in that game, but this one touchdown that he had was one of the most amazing runs that doesn't hit the highlight reels. Every guy on our team missed him on a seven-yard touchdown run where he covered the whole field. He went *zip…zip…zip-zip…zip.*

You couldn't tackle him, and Catlin knew it. Overall, I thought that game was one of the great coaching jobs by Tom Catlin.

Long Hair and Short Stories

Tom Catlin had the respect of every player on that team, but that didn't mean we wouldn't tease him every now and then.

Tom was bald. And one day he walked in wearing a toupee. We were dying with laughter because it didn't look like him. The whole place was abuzz. He kind of had that little strut. He wore it for maybe a week before the jokes became too much to bear (or was it bare?).

When he smiled, it looked like his face was going to crack. He was drier than a piece of balsa wood.

I (Wyman) remember I was so pleased with myself the day I actually made him laugh. It was the kind of crude humor you'd expect from a bunch of guys who play a game for a living.

At midseason one year, we got a new player whose name was Peter Short. Tom and I were standing next to each other on the sideline during the offensive period of practice. Tom was in a jovial mood, and he turned to me, pointed to the roster in his hand, and said, "How'd you like to go through life with that name?"

I said, "Yeah, what about in class when they call out last names first? Catlin, Tom. Short, Peter."

Tom actually chuckled, and I thought, "Yes! I did it! I made Tom Catlin laugh!"

Backup quarterback Sean Salisbury was another guy who could make Tom laugh. Once on the bus en route to the airport, we got hung up in traffic, and there were cars going every which way and a policeman trying to redirect traffic. It was quite a scene, and Tom, who was sitting up front, called back to Sean to describe it in his Howard Cosell voice. Sean started in: "Well, Tom, this cop looks like a rookie out there…" From behind, you could see Tom's entire body shake with laughter. That's when I knew Sean would end up on television someday.

At Northwest College, in the coaches' room, we had a freezer just stuffed with Dove Bars. We called it the Dove Bar Lounge. Chuck loved them. Chuck would have his scotch and be venting about something, Joe Vitt would be cracking jokes, and Catlin would come in, sit down and eat a Dove Bar quietly all by himself. He would sit there and not say a word, smile every once in a while. He always had two.

And Chuck would tease him: "Ah, Tom, won't have a drink, but you'll have two Dove Bars."

Maybe that's why Tom Catlin always seemed so at peace.

The Other Assistants

Joe Vitt is one of the all-time characters in coaching. He was the best storyteller, a stand-up comedian who would make you laugh at the worst times. And he was a guy everyone loved because he was so passionate about football.

He came to the Seahawks in 1982 as the strength coach, but as he said, there wasn't much to being a strength coach back in the 1980s. When Chuck Knox arrived the next year, Joe's primary job became to break down defensive game film for coordinator Tom Catlin.

"When I was the strength coach, there was no cutting edge of strength-coaching," Vitt said in 2005. "It was really kind of a part-time job for me. When I went to Seattle, my main job was to do defensive breakdowns and weigh the guys in and break stuff down on film. The strength stuff probably only took three or four hours a day.

"When Chuck Knox came to Seattle, he was absolutely not going to have a strength coach. Chuck was old-school. He was going to teach guys fundamentals—how to tackle and block—and he really didn't care about lifting weights."

Joe was so important because he was the only one who knew how to break down film. He knew what every formation was called, what every running play was called. And he would put it in the game plan and scouting for the other team. No one else knew how to do it.

In 1986 Joe had testicular cancer, went through chemotherapy, and didn't miss a practice, except when he had surgery. And even then, he wanted people to bring him film so he could watch it and break it down.

They called Joe Vitt "Leash" because he talked really tough like he was going to stand up to Chuck, but when the leash was let loose and he had his chance, he never did it.

Basically Joe was Chuck Knox's boy.

Chuck: "I need a ride to the airport."

Joe: "Okay, Coach."

Chuck: "I need to be picked up."

Joe: "Okay, Coach."

Chuck: "I need you to take this report downstairs for me. I need you to get some film for me."

Joe: "Okay."

One day we were in the coaches' conference room waiting for Chuck to arrive—he was always last. And Joe was fed up. "I'm so tired of this crap," he said. "If Chuck comes in and asks me to do one more thing, I'm not doing it." And he just went off on Chuck until Chuck got there.

When Knox walked into the room, he said, "Joe…"

And Joe jumped to attention and responded, "Yeah, Coach?"

Chuck said, "I need you to run down and take care of this…"

And Joe responded as usual, with an eager, "Okay, Coach," and he ran out and did it.

After that, Rusty Tillman started calling him "Leash."

In our coaches meetings, Joe would always try to crack me (Moyer) and Rusty Tillman up. He would make facial expressions or he would come in with a story about something that happened at practice, and he would imitate the guys involved. Rusty and I would try so hard not to laugh, pinching ourselves and biting our lips. Chuck, who was always serious and stoic in those meetings, would look over at us, and tears would be coming down our faces.

Joe always had an opinion about something.

I (Wyman) bought a house back in Stanford my rookie year. It was built in 1906 and is probably worth $3 million now. But it was kind of a trashed old house, so I bought it for $390,000, which was a lot of money back then.

Joe mocked me for that: "Oh, you're a real genius, Stanford guy, buying a fixer-upper for $390,000. That's a real smart move."

About a year later, he saw me in the training room and asked, "So how's that fixer-upper doing, genius?"

I told him I had sold it nine months later for $470,000, and he shot back, "Oh, you should have kept it longer, you dumbass!" He was right.

Chuckles at My Expense

They say I (Moyer) was the first assistant coach under Chuck Knox to miss a practice. In 1990 I had the flu bad. I had done my work, and we were getting ready to go out to practice. I was in the bathroom, and Joe Vitt said, "You need to go home."

I said, "I'm not going home. Are you nuts? Coaches don't go home."

He said, "You need to go home. You're no use. I'll get your work done tonight. Go home. I'll go talk to Chuck."

So Chuck Knox came down and said, "Hey, Joe said you're not feeling good. He's right. You don't look good. I don't want you getting the players sick. Why don't you go home?"

So I went home and slept it off. When I got to practice the next day, I never heard the end of it.

"I cannot believe you went home," Joe said. "I was just kidding. You're the first coach on Chuck's staff to ever go home sick."

The coaches were asking me if I needed anything—"Can we get you some pillows? Are you comfortable?"

I was a young coach and insecure, and they were having fun messing with me.

Even Chuck got in on the action. "I can't believe you went home. At least suck it up through practice."

And I protested, "But you guys told me not to get the players sick…"

Chuck just shook his head, "Yeah, but I didn't think you'd really go home. I've been coaching 30-plus years, and you're the first assistant I've had who has gone home sick."

Dyer's Undying Passion

Our George Dyer was no poet, but he was a passionate guy who cared about his players very much.

Before he became Seattle's defensive line coach in 1983, he was the defensive coordinator at Arizona State and recruited me (Moyer) to play for the Sun Devils.

On a plane ride while he was recruiting me, we were playing cards, and I was beating him on almost every hand. He seemed so upset, "Darn it, you beat me again!" Well, after I committed to ASU, I don't remember ever beating him again. And I always wondered whether that had just been a recruiting ploy.

When he was recruiting me, he told my mom, "I'll take care of your son. Don't worry." And he was true to his word. He would have me over to his house for dinner, and I became friends with his kids.

I played poorly my junior year and was benched, but Dyer didn't lose confidence in me. I thought about quitting, but he encouraged me to keep working hard, and I ended up reclaiming my starting position my senior year and had a great year.

George was always in a good mood, always happy—"Let's go get 'em!" But he was the most broken-down looking coach you'd ever seen. He had a bad knee, wore these big old-fashioned glasses, and always had chew in and would spit all over.

It was quite a contrast to his wife, a really sharp woman who had a lot going for her. You might say George was overmatched, and he knew it. But every time somebody would say that, he would always respond, "I think I could have done a lot better." And you had to laugh.

George provided a lot of comic relief—some intended and some not.

He would tell the guys he used to play for the Philadelphia Eagles, and the only person who ever seemed to believe it was Terry Taylor: "George, I didn't know you played for the Eagles?!"

An entertaining diversion during the hours and hours of film we used to review was watching people get "taken out" on the sideline by a play that had continued off the field. George was a magnet for those kinds of plays.

If anyone was going to get run over on the sideline, it was going to be George. There were times that if he had just stood still, he would have been fine. But he would take off running and invariably intersect with the collision of players. One time a whole pile of players was headed toward him, so he jumped in the air and folded his legs underneath him in an effort to clear the pile. But the players missed him entirely, and he landed straight down on his knees. It was one of the funniest things I'd ever seen in those film sessions.

One year, George and I (Wyman) drove down to a football camp in Oregon in his little Datsun pickup truck. His son had just gotten into the Naval Academy, so every 15 minutes, George would push in a tape with "Anchors Aweigh" and sing along. He would rewind it and play it again, and then he would rewind it and play it again, and then he would rewind it and play it again. He did that the whole way down.

When he was fired from Detroit in 2003, George was down at the Senior Bowl in Mobile, Alabama. Terry Wooden and I were with him, and he just broke down crying. "I really love my players," he said, "and my players love me."

He was a really loyal guy, and it was sad to see his coaching career—something that meant so much to him—coming to an end. It showed how he felt about it. A lot of coaches do it for the money and are very businesslike, whereas George was very passionate about it and loved his guys, and that's the way he coached.

I think that was the end of coaching for George, but he got in close to 35 years in the league (including zero as a player with the Eagles) and has about 10 grandchildren to coach now.

"That's Not My Job"

Arnie Matsumoto started off as a ball boy in 1987. The Seahawks took him on because he was interested in football. He was a Japanese guy from Hawaii who spoke broken English, but he really wanted to learn.

Bruce Scholtz, Greg Gaines, Keith Butler, and those guys used to take care of Arnie, bring him to the house and everything.

Eventually, Arnie worked his way up to more important tasks. When Joe Vitt was fighting cancer, Arnie took over Vitt's role as the guy who broke down all of the film. And Arnie suddenly became a football expert.

He did know a lot about formations and stuff, but I (Moyer) always thought, "You know nothing about football and you're telling *me* what to do?"

He came from no knowledge of football—he never played and didn't really understand the game. It was like taking a class at a university, where you sit down and start learning from scratch. He actually got pretty good.

But he also got a big head about it. He wanted to be respected like a coach. He was sensitive to any perceived slight.

In 1989 Bruce asked Arnie to get a cleat mat, and Arnie said, "That's not my job anymore." Scholtz was so mad because he had taken care of Arnie, and all of a sudden Arnie was big-timing him.

Once he became the video guy, you could not treat him like he was a servant. But he did his job well, and it was a nice success story for a guy who barely knew English, let alone the language of football, when he first arrived.

Grandpa Munster

Ralph Hawkins was our secondary coach in the 1980s. And from a scheme standpoint in a nickel situation, he ran one of the most complex defenses of that era. We ran a lot of double coverages and disguised them. We had really smart guys in the secondary, so we could do a lot of things. And we showed it in the 1984 season, when we intercepted 38 passes and returned seven of them for touchdowns.

I might not have made the Seahawks' roster if Ralph hadn't lobbied for Chuck to keep me in 1983, when I was an undrafted rookie out of ASU. The other players referred to me as Ralph's son or the token white in the secondary.

A lot of my fellow defensive backs didn't have a lot of respect for Ralph because they thought he didn't like them. Whenever they had an issue, they always sent me to go talk to him.

He looked exactly like Grandpa Munster, and he acted like Don Rickles. He was really abusive, although he usually was joking. But people just didn't understand his brand of humor. He was from the old school, and he said things that were probably inappropriate because he had grown up in a different time.

Ralph also was the greatest joke-teller with the worst punchlines ever; he would always laugh at his jokes before he was finished telling them. When he was serious, we had to be serious; but he joked 90 percent of the time, so it was hard to turn it on and turn it off.

He was the best at dishing it out, but he was the worst at taking it. He used to walk through the lunchroom and take a bite of other people's sandwiches. So one time Brian Bosworth walked over and picked up Ralph's sandwich and took a bite out of it—giving Ralph a so-called taste of his own medicine. Ralph did not like that, and he got really upset at Boz. From then on, Ralph would spit on his sandwiches as a way of discouraging anyone from sampling them.

His quirks aside, Ralph was an incredibly smart man. He would get offers for defensive coordinator positions, and he wanted to feel appreciated, so every year he would ask Chuck Knox if he should take the job that was available.

Chuck would always tell him, "Nah, I think you should stay here a while longer." Then, after the 1988 season, Chuck finally told him, "Maybe it's time."

So he left to become the defensive coordinator of the New York Jets. He was there only for a year and spent the last 12 years of his career as a scout for several teams.

Ralph died at age 69 in September 2004. But I got to see him the previous year when Gary Wright, the Seahawks' longtime PR chief, and I went to his place while we were in Washington, D.C., with the Seahawks. Ralph had Pick's disease, a neurological disorder that causes dementia, and didn't remember a lot. But Gary and I would bring up old stories, and Ralph would soon become his old self as he recalled the good old days with the Seahawks, when he was in charge of one of the best secondaries in the NFL.

Kamikaze Tillman's Teams

Rusty Tillman was one of the best special-teams players of his day when he played for the Washington Redskins. He was known for his kamikaze style, launching his body into the air to break the blocking wedge on kickoffs.

He took that same passion and expectation to his players when he coached special teams in Seattle. He felt special teams were absolutely as important as offense and defense—after all, they accounted for 20 percent of the plays each game. He was a master of motivation, and we were always up there in the top 10 in special teams under Rusty.

On Monday mornings, the whole team watched film of special teams. So you would be praised or called out in front of the whole team. If you played special teams, that was a scary day.

Rusty had an award system he called "Dash for Cash," which rewarded players for making big special-teams plays.

For every tackle inside the 20-yard line, you'd get $50. If special teams forced the other team to start inside the 5-yard line, everyone on that kicking team got $50. If you made two blocks on a kick or punt return, you got $50. If you blocked a punt or kick or scored, you got $100.

We only got paid if we won, though. And if you had a penalty on special teams, you wouldn't get the money you had earned; it would go to charity.

On Mondays, Rusty would call up the players who had done well and list the things they had done, and the whole team would burst out in applause, and Chuck would be standing there smiling. It was like you had won the lottery.

Special-teams players never got much credit. But Mondays after wins were great because special-teams players got recognized and rewarded for their performances. And the offensive and defensive starters who didn't play on special teams were jealous as they watched all of this cash being handed out. The recognition was more important than the cash. But we made good use of the money by going out to celebrate Monday night.

In one game, I (Moyer) had tallied $600—I was counting as I earned it—and then they called holding on me on one return. I tried to talk Rusty out of it Monday: "Come on, Rusty, that wasn't holding." But he wouldn't waver. So when he announced my name, he said, "And $600 goes to Paul Moyer…to charity."

When the salary cap was created in 1993, they said the Dash for Cash would be subject to the cap. So they had to end it. It was a bummer when that went away.

Rusty's coaching style was to challenge people. If he felt he could bully you, he would keep it up until you challenged him back.

I (Wyman) loved Rusty on a personal level, and he was a great coach, but there were times that I hated him. I learned that all you had to do was stand up to him one time. He was yelling at me on the sideline during a game once, and I cussed him out. On the bus after the game, he turned to me as if he were going to try to back me down again. And I cussed him out again. Our relationship was different after that.

Mike Tice never learned that, and Rusty had Mike by the balls because of it. Rusty would jump all over Tice, and Mike would say, "Oh, Rusty, I'm sorry."

When Tice became coach of the Minnesota Vikings, he hired Rusty to coach the Vikings' special teams. And then the roles were reversed.

chapter 9
Seasonal Stories

Steve Largent catches his 100th career TD pass against the Bengals at Cincinnati in 1989, breaking the 44-year-old record for TD catches set by Don Hutson and giving the Seahawks a 24–17 win.
Courtesy AP/Wide World Photos

In 1986 We Bombed Out

In 1986 we had just lost 34–7 to Cincinnati. It was our fourth straight loss, and we were getting blown out. We hadn't scored more than one touchdown in any of those games. We'd just gotten the crap kicked out of us. And, on top of that, people wanted to kill us.

At the airport in Cincinnati, we were sitting on the plane ready to fly back to Seattle, and all of a sudden we got a bomb threat. We ended up having to wait in the hangar, cold and tired and hungry. The dogs were sniffing around. We were freezing our butts off.

It was comical at that point, and we just said, "Well, it can't get any worse than this."

We kind of relaxed and came out of the funk. We won our final five games and just missed the playoffs at 10–6.

We averaged eight points in the four-game losing streak, but our offense could not be stopped in the final five games, when we averaged 33.4 points. We were the hottest team in the NFL, and no one wanted to play us. A lot of fans still say that was our best team of that era and that if we had made the playoffs we would have won the Super Bowl.

In 1989 a Grudge Match

I (Wyman) remember being really fired up before that game. The Bengals were dogging us in the paper and talking about how they were going to kick our asses.

They were upset over the playoff game from the season before, when we faked injuries to slow down their offense. Chuck Knox really played up the bulletin-board stuff, where they were saying we had no chance to win that game.

Everyone was predicting us to lose—even some guy I ran into on the elevator in the hotel. He looked at me and asked if I played for the Seahawks. When I said yes, he said, "I don't think you guys have a chance against the Bengals."

My mood changed from semi-friendly to pregame intolerant in a millisecond. I snapped back, "Yeah? I think we're gonna kick the shit out of them!" He backed away from me a step and trained his eyes on the door. Poor bastard. He thought he was just making casual conversation.

From the start, the game felt like a grudge match from high school or college.

The first drive, they came out and went all the way down the field to the 5-yard line. Just then, a sheet of snow started to come down. First-and-goal on the 5, we ended up stuffing them four times in a row. Nesby Glasgow and I stuffed Ickey Woods on fourth down. We were so fired up after that, and we knew we were going to win.

Steve Largent, who had missed seven games and was in his final season, finally set the NFL record with his 100th touchdown catch, and we ended up winning a very good game, 24–17.

At one point, our offense was backed up toward our own end zone, and Bengals fans started pelting our guys with snowballs. Sam Wyche, the Bengals coach, grabbed a microphone and told the fans to stop throwing snowballs, punctuating the demand with, "You don't live in Cleveland. You live in Cincinnati!"

They were doing that because they were so upset about how we slowed their offense in that 1988 playoff game.

After the game, the Bengals were bitter about losing, and they turned the hot water off on us. It was the coldest shower I've ever taken in my life, like it came right out of the river. There's just no other explanation for that. You always hear rumors about teams that do that to other teams, and I'm sure that was it.

In 1990 We Waved a White Flag

In 1990 we went from Ground Chuck to the run-and-shoot. The new craze in the NFL was the run-and-shoot offense. Chuck was a traditionalist: I formation, run twice, throw on third.

Chuck relented and let offensive coordinator John Becker incorporate the run-and-shoot. But I've never seen Chuck as uncomfortable during practice and going into a season as he was in the 1990 season. Chuck was very skeptical.

We spent the entire preseason working on it and had enough success that Chuck was comfortable going into the opening game with the offense.

But then we got shut out 17–0 in Chicago. We looked like a high school offense playing an NFL defense.

And as fast as you could say "run-and-shoot," Chuck shot it down. The next day, he walked into the meeting and said, "Well, that's the last I ever want to see of that run-and-shoot." So we scrapped it right then and there and went back to what Chuck was comfortable with: I formation, run, run, pass.

We came back home to play the Los Angeles Raiders, and we lost because the referees blew a call. Swervin' Mervyn Fernandez didn't get both feet in on a 45-yard catch, but the refs let the play go and then didn't review it.

That was the maddest I've ever seen Chuck Knox. He said, "Here we have the NFL with all of its sophisticated technology. How simple would this be? You've got a white flag to signal overturn, you've got a red flag to let it stand.

"Here we've got these senile old guys making million-dollar decisions, and they can't even make a simple call like this when he was clearly out of bounds."

Back then, when the guys in the booth saw something, they were supposed to call down to the refs on the field to correct it. They didn't have the challenge back then like they do now.

The guy actually was reviewing it upstairs, but he had not told the referee, Jerry Markbreit. So Markbreit let the Raiders run another play, and that was that. We were ahead 10–3 in the third quarter at the time, and they tied it up with a touchdown a few plays later. We lost 17–13.

Chuck was upset about that because it was preventable. It wasn't a judgment call, like pass interference or holding. He got a call from the NFL that week, and they apologized. Chuck said it was "the most meaningless apology in the world," because what could you do? Nothing.

We lost that one, and then we lost an overtime game in Denver the next week, so we started 0–3.

That season was probably one of Chuck's greatest coaching jobs because even at that point Chuck was still up for the fight. He felt we could still make the playoffs. And he showed it by how upset he got about that blown call in the Raiders game.

It was his energy. Chuck always told us, "Don't get too high and don't get too low," meaning don't get too excited about a win and don't get too upset about a loss because the season was long. He was a pretty even-tempered man and wanted us to act the same way. But that season you could see the energy and emotion that he usually hid. There was pressure to win that year, and Chuck was out to prove he was still a great coach. I think the whole team felt the pressure coming into the season, but Chuck took the pressure off us and put it on himself.

It worked—almost. We bounced back and won five of our last six games to finish 9–7. Then we had to wait to find out whether we got into the playoffs.

We needed the Pittsburgh Steelers to beat the Houston Oilers, in which case the Steelers would have won the AFC Central and we would have edged out the Bengals for the wild-card. It looked pretty good for us, too, because Warren Moon was injured and wasn't going to play for Houston.

ESPN wanted to show a split screen of Seahawks and Bengals watching the Oilers-Steelers game. So Joe Cain and I (Wyman) went down to the KOMO studios and watched as Cody Carlson came in for Moon and had a huge game. Houston won 34–13.

On one screen were the Bengals cheering and celebrating at Boomer Esiason's bar in Cincinnati. On the other were Joe and I, looking downcast and gloomy in a little box of a room in the KOMO studios. The whole country saw our misery that night as our season ended.

In 1992 Our Offense Was Offensive

In 1992 we lost to the Raiders 20–3 in Los Angeles. We held them to 188 yards in offense, but *our* offense could do nothing. We had 159 yards and only 10 first downs. It was never fourth-and-two or fourth-and-three. It was always fourth-and-10, fourth-and-25, fourth-and-30.

It was typical of how the season had gone. It was our ninth loss in 10 games, the sixth time we had not scored a touchdown, and the fifth time we had scored three points or less. We had the worst offense in NFL history at the time.

The day after the Raiders game, we were in our defensive meeting, and Tom Catlin was just reaming us—not screaming and yelling at us, but simply telling us what we could have done better. We all just sat there, took it, and admitted, "Yeah, we made some mistakes. We could have played better." We weren't perfect, but that's how Tom was. He didn't care what we had done; he wanted us to go out and try to be the best we could.

I (Wyman) didn't think it was anything out of the ordinary. That was just how it went in Tom's meetings. I wasn't beating myself up about it.

After the meeting, I went into the bathroom, and offensive linemen Andy Heck and Darrick Brilz were talking about the game. The line had given up seven sacks, and one of them said, "Oh, I had you graded out to a B+." The other guy said, "Yeah, that's where I had you. I thought a lot of things were out of your control."

They were actually trying to justify why the offense had been so bad. And I thought, "Isn't that a bitch?" I just came out of a meeting where we were criticized for not doing enough despite having a great game…and then to hear what was coming from the other side…

I heard that all year long.

But our offense was so bad that year, my running joke was I could never sit long enough to finish a cup of Gatorade.

When we were getting ready to play Kansas City the next week, I was on the scout-team defense in practice one day. Our offense ran this running play, and I came up in the hole and formed up on running back Chris Warren. I was right there to make the tackle.

Our line coach, Hudson Houck, told the offense, "Okay, good job."

I said, "Coach, what about this guy? I didn't get blocked."

And he replied, "Oh, we'll run right through you."

I thought, "Oh, really? That hasn't been the case all year."

But that's the attitude the offense had that year.

Tom Flores somehow managed to keep that team together. There was never any finger-pointing or dissension on that team. Flores might have done the best coaching job of his career that year because, on a team that probably had the biggest contrast ever in offensive and defensive talent, there was never any bickering or fighting.

The offense had seven games where it didn't reach 200 yards. We had the potential to take a halftime lead seven times, yet the offense would give the ball back in the final two minutes. We turned the ball over at least twice in every game and six times in that 24–14 loss to Kansas City.

We lost to Philly in overtime. They had 95 plays, and we sacked them eight times. In a 20–17 loss, we had 87 yards of offense, and coordinator Larry Kennan credited the Eagles defense for being so good. He had done the same thing when we had 82 yards against Dallas earlier that year. According to him, it had nothing to do with how bad our offense was, even though we statistically had the most inept offense in team history and the lowest-scoring offense in league history.

In 1994 We Were Finished When Frier Was Paralyzed

There was a lot of promise coming into the 1994 season. We had Rick Mirer at quarterback, with one year under his belt. He looked like he was the real deal after his rookie year in 1993.

We started out 3–1, beating Washington and the Raiders on the road and then Pittsburgh at home. Those were three teams considered to be Super Bowl contenders. And we averaged 32 points in those three wins. After two horrible seasons, we felt we had turned the franchise around.

But one thing we didn't have was depth, and injuries started to hit us. Mirer started to have sophomore blues, which later became career blues. Defenses finally figured out how to stop Mirer: they would put a spy (a linebacker or safety would be waiting for him to break the pocket and run) on him because he scrambled a lot. Teams would scout our tendencies, and they would take away our primary receiver. Usually when that happens, a quarterback will start to scan the field and work to his second and third passing options, but Rick was more comfortable tucking the ball in his arm and running. And the spy defense negated Mirer's best attributes, his feet.

So the injury bug hit, and Mirer couldn't bail us out, and we went into a spiral and ended up losing six straight.

It was miserable. This team was very fragile when it came to winning. We had come off 2-14 and 6-10 seasons and were accustomed to losing. So when the six-game skid came, it was depressing to go to work. It was like a dark cloud was hanging over the team. But somehow Tom Flores kept the team together, and we finally got out of that slide.

We had won two games and gotten to 5-7, and we were feeling pretty good about ourselves again. We had games against Indianapolis, at Houston, against the Raiders, and at Cleveland. We really thought we could win our next three games and have a chance at the playoffs going into the final game. We had a home game coming up against a weak Indianapolis team that we had lost to earlier in the season, so revenge was on our minds, as well.

But three days before we were to play the Colts, defensive lineman Mike Frier was paralyzed in a car accident in which running back Lamar Smith was driving and our starting running back, Chris Warren, was also a passenger.

They were heading home after a late night on the town, and they hit a telephone pole near the team complex. A car speaker fell forward and hit Frier in the back of the neck and paralyzed him.

That was as low as it gets. When one of your fellow teammates has fallen, you're not prepared. You don't know how to react. It was like a death in the family. It really affected our emotions going into the game against the Colts. Not only did we have no emotion, but the crowd—fewer than 40,000 people—had no emotion. It was like we were at practice; it didn't feel like a game. In a game, we should have played like warriors for Mike, but we ended up playing like it was practice. We lost 31–19.

We were in disbelief. We couldn't believe we played with such a lack of emotion, and we couldn't believe we had lost to an inferior team. I don't think the team had time to build back up emotionally from such a devastating injury to a teammate. It's the type of injury every player fears but no one talks about. That was the lowest point in my NFL career.

Somehow we won the next one at Houston, 16–14—we definitely had the run-and-shoot offense mastered defensively. But then we lost a heartbreaker to the Raiders, 17–16, and that's when I knew we (the coaches) were all going to get fired because we were out of the playoffs again.

We lost three of our last four and finished 6–10, and the Frier incident drained us. There was no emotion, no fight, we walked around like zombies. It was like a death around the complex. And in the typical class that Ken Behring showed after such an emotional year, he fired Tom Flores after only three seasons.

chapter 10
The Holmgren Era

Mike Holmgren brought success and smiles to Seattle when he was hired by the Seahawks in 1999.
Courtesy AP/Wide World Photos

Holmgren's Teams

When Mike Holmgren was hired in 1999, he was viewed as the savior for the Seahawks. He had been to two Super Bowls and won one, and he was considered *the* genius in the NFL at the time.

Expectations were high. We thought they had a pretty good team. They had Ricky Watters at running back. They let Warren Moon go, but Jon Kitna had played a lot the previous year, and they signed Glenn Foley.

Foley started the opener because Kitna was hurt, and the Hawks ended up losing to a bad Detroit team, 28–20. The sentiment immediately became, "Here we go again."

But Kitna came back, and they won eight of their next nine games. The big one was in Green Bay on *Monday Night Football*. It was Mike Holmgren's return to the place where he had become a hero and had a street named after him. His Seahawks killed Green Bay 27–7. That was the highlight of the season. It was their fifth win in six games, and they would run their record to 8–2 before the warts started to show.

They lost five of their last six regular-season games and backed into the playoffs on the final weekend when Kansas City lost to Oakland. Then the questions started. Was Kitna going to be the guy at quarterback? He completed just 54 percent of passes that season and had a high interception rate.

Fans loved Jon because he was another one of those unheralded free-agent gems the Seahawks had always seemed to find at quarterback, like Jim Zorn and Dave Krieg. But Holmgren didn't know if he was the quarterback of the future.

Because Holmgren had an eight-year contract, he was afforded the opportunity to rebuild and put the team together the way he wanted. The next year, the Seahawks went 6–10, and that's when you knew Kitna wasn't the guy. Holmgren tried Brock Huard, too. And he decided he wanted to set this team up his way. He wanted to build what he'd had in Green Bay.

So in 2001 he traded for Matt Hasselbeck, a Packers quarterback who knew his system. When Matt came to Seattle, you could see his ability. He had great feet and a nice release, and he was accurate. He was just a fraction off. He just wasn't letting it go. It was the pressure of it. He was the savior, and they were trying to say, "He's not the savior." He had never started before, and it showed.

Matt wasn't playing at a level then that would afford him a chance to win. But Trent Dilfer came in and won all four starts when Matt was hurt or ineffective.

When Holmgren decided to re-sign Dilfer and make him the starting quarterback in 2002, it was the right decision because Holmgren needed to take pressure off Hasselbeck, who had been brought in as the savior and wasn't ready to be.

Obviously, the thought of going more than two years in a row with a losing record was more than Mike could handle. So he decided to go with Dilfer. But Dilfer tore his Achilles tendon against Dallas in the seventh game, and Matt had to take over again. This time, you could see the weight was off his shoulders. He played free and just took off.

The Seahawks were hot at the end of that season. They scored 39, 24, 20, 30, 30, and 31 points to end it. They won four of those games and finished 7–9. And for the first time you thought they might be ready to win in the playoffs. It took four years to build a team that was a legitimate division contender.

After they beat the Chargers 31–28 in overtime in San Diego to end the season, there was a happy feeling around the team. It was almost as if they had won a playoff game. You could sense the confidence that they felt they had arrived.

They were young and had a swagger about them. They were loaded on offense, with Shaun Alexander, Koren Robinson, and Steve Hutchinson—all guys drafted in the first round by Holmgren.

But people were still asking, "Where are the playoff wins?" Because after four years, Holmgren had the same record (31–33) that Dennis Erickson had put together before he was fired. People would call in to our radio show and ask what the difference was. The difference was that Holmgren had gone to the playoffs and had two winning seasons. And this team looked ready to contend.

People were questioning whether Holmgren should be the guy. People who knew football knew based on how 2002 ended that the Seahawks were ready. But it was odd that some fans thought he shouldn't be there.

In 2003 the Seahawks went to Green Bay for the playoffs, and the better team did not win that day. Everyone knows about Hasselbeck saying, "We want the ball, and we're gonna score," and the interception in overtime. But that loss was not that bad because you could see the Seahawks were right there.

More disappointing was the 2004 playoff game, when the Seahawks lost at home to the St. Louis Rams, 27–20. After that loss, it felt like the Seahawks weren't a good team. It was a very inconsistent season.

The dropped passes that year were an epidemic. The picture of that whole season was Matt crumpled on the 5-yard line at the end of the playoff game, frustrated with a season in which his guys couldn't catch the ball for him.

Even on Hasselbeck's last throw, Bobby Engram couldn't haul it in for the touchdown. The whole year, Matt never got frustrated. He would make all of these great throws, but his guys—mainly Robinson and Darrell Jackson—would drop them.

After 2003, 2004 felt like a step back.

In 2005 Tim Ruskell became president and made a defensive overhaul. Then the offense turned into magic, becoming the top-scoring unit in the league. Everything came together that year as they advanced to the Super Bowl.

The Coach and the Quarterback

Hasselbeck is a really fine quarterback and more athletic than people give him credit for.

I (Wyman) think the fact that he's a bald, white guy makes people think he's not an athlete. But he disproved that for me

Mike Holmgren introduces the media to the Seahawks' new starting quarterback, Matt Hasselbeck, at a news conference in March 2001.
Courtesy AP/Wide World Photos

once and for all in the 2005 NFC Championship Game against Carolina. He ran a naked bootleg, and Julius Peppers, one of the best athletes in the league, was right in his face, but Matt juked him and got around the corner.

Matt is way ahead of his time maturity-wise. He has the wisdom and perspective of a much older person, and I think that really helps him on the field. His downfall seems to be the same things that affected Brett Favre. Matt's not quite the gunslinger that Favre was, but when things go south, he has a tendency to force plays that aren't there. Other than that, he's very consistent.

So much of that comes from Holmgren. Without Mike's tutelage, I'm not sure Matt would be as good a quarterback as he is. The way Mike has brought him along and developed his skills, like he did with Brett Favre, is something else. Along with the Super Bowl victory with the Packers and another appearance with the Seahawks in 2005, his quarterback coaching skills are what make Holmgren a Hall of Fame coach.

Holmgren could be tough on his players. But if you played to high level and could handle criticism, he was a great coach and great to be around. He's a motivator and knows how he wants to motivate. Mike made players better than they were.

In addition, Mike is a great play-caller. He's a natural. If you let him just go with his feel and his gut, it usually works out. He's like an artist. He does it more off the feel and flow of the game as opposed to statistics. A lot of times he doesn't follow a system or a rhyme or reason; he just goes with what feels right.

The Polarizing Running Back

Shaun Alexander was a lightning rod in Seattle. Some people loved him, and some people did not.

Those who loved him would say he had a real nose for the end zone and ran hard once he was inside the 20-yard line. But those who didn't like him would say he didn't run hard between the 20s.

Those who loved him would say he's one of the most durable backs in league history, having never missed a game in his first six seasons. Those who didn't like him would say he shied away from contact, wouldn't block anybody, and ran out of bounds, leaving yards on the table.

Those who loved him would say he was the NFL rushing leader in 2005 and a major reason the Seahawks went to the Super Bowl. Those who didn't like him would say he ran hard in

2005 only because he wanted a big contract, and once he got paid, he didn't perform.

For those reasons, Shaun was one of the more controversial players in franchise history.

And all of this never really surfaced until the last game of the 2004 season. On a fourth-and-goal play on the Atlanta Falcons 1-yard line, Mike Holmgren worked his magical play-calling ability by calling a quarterback sneak when the whole world was expecting the ball to go to Shaun. The play worked, and the victory over the Falcons gave the Seahawks home-field advantage in the first round of the playoffs.

But that call also left Shaun one yard short of a stake in the NFL rushing title (tied with Curtis Martin). After the game, Shaun said it felt like Mike Holmgren "stabbed him in the back." His comments were soon explained and washed over; but for most people, it gave a glimpse into what is really most important to Shaun.

Shaun rushed for more yards than anyone ever had in Mike Holmgren's offense, and then he went and said Mike backstabbed him?

Those comments were quickly forgotten the next year when Shaun ran for 1,880 yards and scored 27 touchdowns. But there was speculation that since he was on the eve of his thirties and wouldn't be as productive once he got his big contract, it would be a big mistake to re-sign him. In March 2006 he signed a $62 million contract. That season he rushed for 896 yards and scored only seven touchdowns. In 2007 he ran for 716 yards and scored just four times.

More so than the average fan, his peers and NFL insiders had a hard time with Shaun at times. Not that he's a bad guy. But they didn't like the things he would say or the way he would play.

I have a hard time watching him surrender once he figures out that a play is going nowhere. When he goes down with very little contact, I call it his "okay, okay, you got me" move. And the fact that he either won't or can't block or catch is a little annoying. Both of them are things that are mostly associated with desire among players.

Shaun Alexander shakes off a Jacksonville Jaguars defender in October 2001. Alexander rushed 31 times for 176 yards and two touchdowns in just his second NFL start. Courtesy AP/Wide World Photos

He also was seen as being a little too flippant after some losses. In 2007 the Seahawks were trying to set up the winning field goal late in the game against the Arizona Cardinals. Hasselbeck made a "dummy" audible that everyone except Shaun heard. Matt and Shaun ran into each other and fumbled the ball, which was recovered by Arizona. It cost them the game. Afterward, Shaun laughingly recounted the play, comparing it to an old movie where a guy doesn't want the ball and runs around looking for someone to hand it to.

During the 2007 season, the fans started questioning him, too, and his running style was seen as a self-preservation thing. True, his avoidance of contact probably helped him stay very healthy. Before missing nine games in 2006 and 2007, he had not missed a game for six seasons. But players and fans alike saw him as a sellout and began to think, "Hey, we needed those yards. Why didn't you try harder?"

Once the fans turned on him, I began to get defensive of Shaun. After the Seahawks' playoff victory against the Redskins in January 2008, a caller on the postgame radio show ridiculed Shaun for the way he got up off the ground after a 13-yard gain. I responded, "Shaun just had a pretty good game, we're going to the second round of the NFL playoffs, and you're worried about how Shaun Alexander got up off of the ground?"

It's insane that he gets a bad rap almost as if he's a bad guy. He's a great dad and husband and a model citizen. What's not to like about him as a person?

But there are a few things that he does and says that sometimes make you think that he may not be the best teammate in the world.

At the end of the day, you have to look at Shaun Alexander like this: he was very productive and helped the Seahawks win a lot of games, and there is no use lamenting the kind of player that he was not. He was not going to catch the ball out of the backfield or stick his face in front of a blitzing linebacker, but he was going to pick up a lot of yards and score a lot of touchdowns.

When it was all over, when the team let him go in 2008, Shaun Alexander left as perhaps the most polarizing player in team history.

"He's Just a Guard"

After the Seahawks lost Super Bowl XL in February 2006, they re-signed Shaun Alexander but were unable to keep All-Pro guard Steve Hutchinson because they tendered him as a transition player, and the Minnesota Vikings swooped in with a contract the Seahawks couldn't match.

The contract, which averaged $7 million a year over seven seasons, required Hutchinson to be the highest-paid lineman on his team or else his entire $49 million contract would be guaranteed. In Minnesota, no other lineman was even close to $7 million per year; but in Seattle, All-Pro left tackle Walter Jones was making more than that. And the Seahawks were not willing to guarantee $49 million to a guard, so they let Hutch go.

We think the entire fiasco was the NFL's fault. The Seahawks told Hutch they were willing to match any offer he got, but no one saw that coming.

The spirit of the rule was that you should have a chance to match the contract. That's a great way to show that the original team cares about the player and is willing to pay what everyone thinks he is worth. When the Vikings wrote the clause that made it impossible to match, the NFL allowed the Vikings to rewrite that entire rule.

The commissioner could have come in and nixed that contract, making it null and void. The spirit of the rule is that you should be able to keep a star as long as you pay him. But it was wrong that the NFL didn't do anything.

Blame the NFL, but don't blame the Seahawks. They told him they were going to match it.

You also can blame Hutch for signing a deal he had to know the Seahawks wouldn't match. I (Wyman) think Hutch was insulted they didn't make him a bigger priority.

Mike Reinfeldt, former lead contract negotiator for the Seahawks, told me there are seven positions you pay, and they are the guys on the perimeter—quarterbacks, running backs, receivers, outside linebackers, offensive tackles, defensive ends,

Steve Hutchinson blocks during the Seahawks' NFC Championship Game in Seattle in January 2006. Courtesy AP/Wide World Photos

and cornerbacks. You don't pay your middle-of-the-field guys, especially guards.

And I kept saying that all during 2006. He's just a guard. You could plug anybody in there. But sure enough, now we know how important Hutch is. He is amazing. He's not your typical offensive lineman.

If you watched him on film coming out of college, he should have been a top-10 pick. Instead he fell all the way to 17, where the Seahawks got him. If you watch him on film, he was the best lineman to come out of that draft. Athletically, the way he moved, the way he mauled people, he was a great guard. But you said, "He's just a guard."

During the Super Bowl season, Hutch was a team guy. But when Super Bowl XL was over, self-orientation jumped out immediately. We were at a party, and he said, "I may not be coming back." And I (Moyer) thought, "You're part of a line that could be one of the best in league history, and you could be doing this for another five or six years." It struck me as odd that he thought there was a possibility he might not come back.

I (Wyman) don't think it was about the money; it was about the respect. The team had a chance to do something earlier, but it didn't happen for whatever reason.

At the party, someone from the team said, "Hey, we really want you back." And Hutch said, "Well, then why didn't you do something earlier?"

When it's all said and done, I think most people will say Walter Jones was one of the best offensive tackles in the history of the game. And maybe six or seven years from now, people will say the same thing about Hutch.

Character and Characters

In the 1980s, we had some guys on the team who were there because they looked good and had good times in the 40-yard dash. Back then, personal character was third behind athleticism and playmaking ability when judging football players the team might want to draft or sign.

Holmgren seemed to make some of the same mistakes when he was the general manager. His two biggest errors were using first-round draft picks on receiver Koren Robinson (2001) and Jerramy Stevens (2002).

Both had their share of well-publicized, alcohol-related problems during their time with the Seahawks, and Holmgren continually gave them extra chances to prove they had cleaned up their acts. But once Tim Ruskell became president in 2005, he cut Robinson. And a year later he let Stevens leave via free agency.

At practice, I (Wyman) used to marvel at the pure athletic talent Koren Robinson had. I always wished you could unscrew one guy's head and screw it on another guy's body.

Contrast them with Shaun, who was great off the field but questionable on the field. You couldn't depend on Jerramy and Koren off the field. But they kept getting opportunities because they were very likable, engaging guys and great athletes. Some people have addiction problems that some people don't understand because they are willing to risk millions of dollars. One side of you feels bad for them. The other side says, "How can you do this to yourself?"

Stevens was two weeks away from free agency in 2007, and he went from a five-year, $20 million contract to making minimum salary because he got arrested for drunk driving again.

You just can't count on people who make such bad decisions.

No one goes out and says, "I'm going to go out tonight and get drunk, get arrested, and cost myself, oh, $18 million." You have to be sick to do that.

With the money players are paid now, you're talking about generational wealth—your grandkids' grandkids will have money. In light of that, to make these kinds of decisions doesn't make sense. It makes you realize how powerful the demons they're fighting are.

chapter 11
Numbers Games

Many consider Walter Jones among the best offensive tackles to ever play the game.

Weigh-In Day

We had to weigh in on Fridays, and we were fined $50 for every pound we were overweight. The things we would do to try to lose the weight were ridiculous.

It was the stupidest thing ever. If you were six pounds over the night before, you would go in early. First of all, you would take a dump. Then you would go into the steam room. And you wouldn't eat anything. And by the morning meeting, everyone was practically anemic.

People got there at 6:00 AM to sweat in the sauna and run to make weight like a wrestler would.

Patrick Hunter, who had 3 percent body fat, would drink some stuff out of a green bottle that would give him diarrhea Thursday night. He would come in at 6:00 AM Friday and hit the sauna. He would spend half the morning in the bathroom, trying to get under weight.

It was all about losing water weight. Cortez Kennedy was the king of that. Tez was 320 pounds and probably carried 40 pounds of water weight at any one time. He'd come in and sit in the sauna starting at about 6:00 AM. By the time the rest of us got there, the entire locker room smelled like whatever Tez had eaten the night before.

Chick Harris, our running backs coach, was the official weigher. He saw us try and cheat Weigh-in Day with every trick we could come up with.

We recalibrated the scale. Or we pulled a trick where someone would hold his hand out from behind Chick, and the person on the scale would put his finger on the teammate's hand to lower his weight. We would practice this beforehand so you didn't come in 10 pounds under weight.

We couldn't wait until weigh-in was over because Friday was doughnut day, and rookies had to bring the doughnuts. All the guys who came in early to work off the extra five pounds would end up devouring the doughnuts.

And after practice, they would bring in Ezell's chicken. Not just a few drumsticks, but a frickin' feast. Ezell would bring in the rolls and the corn on the cob and the cole slaw and about 200 dead chickens. It was an all-you-can-eat buffet.

One year, I (Moyer) came in with around 5 percent body fat, stronger and faster than I had ever been.

One day, Chuck Knox said, "I noticed your weight is 218." I said, "Yeah, I worked out hard, Coach."

Then he asked, "What did you weigh last year?" I said, "202." And then he said, "I want you down to 205."

So I starved myself for the next month to get down from 218 to the opening-season target weight of 205. My body fat shot to about 8 percent. I slowed down because I just wasn't as strong.

One year I (Wyman) was up to 250 or so and was listed at 245. So I mustered the courage to go into Chuck's office to ask for a higher weight. He paused with a look on his face as if he were doing a math formula and then said, "Okay, your new weight is...246." He gave me one single, extra pound.

It got even worse after Chuck joined a bunch of coaches in a Slim-Fast Weight Loss Challenge in 1990. He lost 63 pounds, won the contest, and came to camp looking like a bobblehead. He was already a stickler on weight; but after that, it was hell for the rest of us because he became so self-righteous about it: "If I can do it, you can do it."

Why did we put ourselves through that misery when we could have just paid the $150 or $200 for being a few pounds over official weight? It was pride and a competitive thing. We wanted to prove we could do it. And we didn't want to disappoint Chuck.

Chuck would announce everyone's fines in the Friday morning meeting. I (Wyman) remember it being the first order of business, and for whatever reason, you did not want to get mentioned. Now that I'm away from it, I don't really know why. But at the time it was horrifying to have Chuck mention you in that portion of his morning talk—way worse than the money itself.

We were like beauty contestants. We would be checking ourselves out in the mirror, asking things like, "Do these pants make my butt look big?"

Can you imagine practicing twice a day in camp and starving yourself so you could lose 13 pounds when you had nothing to give? I (Moyer) would get the shakes during practice because my blood-sugar level would drop so fast. The trainers would end up giving me sugar pills and gum to help.

So, to sum up the process on Fridays, it was: arrive early, sweat off water weight all morning in the sauna, eat doughnuts so you don't pass out at practice, and then after practice replace all of the water weight you lost with greasy fried chicken.

Then we'd go run over to TGI Friday's and drink two pitchers of beer. So, after coming in at 198 pounds on Friday, by Sunday you would weigh 212. Because you ate so much, you literally felt fat.

John L. Williams and James Jones and sometimes Patrick Hunter and Kenny Easley would wear plastic pullovers under their jerseys and tape the sleeves shut around their wrists so they would sweat even more during practice.

Nutritionists and weight coaches now would tell them, "All you're going to do is start cramping up."

We just didn't understand nutrition and body fat the way they do today.

It was all about the numbers on the scale. As far as we were concerned, it had absolutely nothing to do with football, but Chuck obviously had his reasons.

Money Matters

In the 1980s, payday in the NFL was not like it is today. There were no direct deposits. We had to do it the old-fashioned way: walk upstairs and ask for it. Payday wasn't always a day you looked forward to.

Chuck Knox wanted you to have to go up the stairs and past his office. He wanted you to feel like you earned your check. And you had to literally go up to Mickey Loomis, our team accountant, and he would hand out your check.

Mickey became the guy everybody didn't like because of that. As guys would trudge upstairs to get paid, with slings around shoulders or braces on knees or wraps around badly sprained ankles, we would just think, "What? We have to go up there and prove to a bean counter that we deserve to be paid? You think we didn't earn this check?"

Chuck didn't want to be that guy, but he wanted that type of atmosphere for us. Everything was done for a reason in that organization. Not to say he was a puppet, but Mickey played that role really, really well. He was the guy who handed you the check, and he made you feel like a loser at times. But that was part of Chuck's master plan.

Mickey acted like the money was his. In 1988, when we went to the playoffs, I (Wyman) got a lot of bonuses—about 30 percent more than my base salary. I was proud of reaching those incentives because they were based on individual and team performance. But Mickey looked at the check and said, "Geez, all of this money we're paying you, we might as well have Fredd Young back here." And I said, "Mickey, just hand over the check. Why you gotta beat me up for it?"

There were times when, if I (Moyer) had a really bad game, I wouldn't even go get it. I would wait a couple of weeks until I had a better game to go get it.

One time I (Wyman) had a sock drawer full of three checks, and I finally got a financial advisor who told me, "You might want to bring those in and start earning some interest on them."

At the end of 1989, I (Moyer) tithed $20,000 to Antioch Bible Church. At the time, that was a lot of money, but my wife and I had never done it before and we believed it was God's money and that He would reward us 100 times over in another way—not necessarily monetarily.

A week later, I thought, "Wow, that kind of stung the wallet a little bit even though it felt good to do."

But a short while later, I was going through my pay stubs and financial stuff to do taxes, and I came across a $30,000 check I hadn't cashed.

I said to my wife, "Heather, look, God did give back—and $10,000 more!"

That $20,000 tithe had been a significant amount of money to us, and we felt really good about giving it, but when I stumbled across the uncashed $30,000 check, it was one of those things where we just looked at each other and said, "How weird is that?"

Some people would take it the other way and say, "You're a frickin' idiot! How do you not cash a $30,000 check?"

It was a good savings plan.

That just shows that we didn't care about the money. Guys like us who really loved the game—what we cared about was doing a good job. And that was my biggest concern. You'd gladly misplace that $30,000 check to not let a guy get open downfield. It was those kinds of things that really concerned you.

I (Wyman) remember one time in 1989, Darren Comeaux, who played linebacker next to me, told me how much money I was making. He was talking about money, and I said, "Yeah, I think I'm making $225,000." And he goes, "No, you're making $255,000."

I said, "I am?" I didn't know.

It wasn't about the money at all. It was about your pride and doing a good job. When that game film went around the league, I really cared about that. I really cared about not getting called out in the film review after games. One of the most quiet, prideful moments is sitting in film review and having a guy like Tom Catlin tell you you did a good job in front of everybody else.

In 1994, after I (Moyer) had learned a little about investing and was an assistant coach, I was in the locker room, and Carlton Gray and a bunch of guys were talking about investments.

"Yeah, I've got it in savings. I'm not giving it to anybody. They'll lose it."

What struck me was how difficult it is to come from college and make all of this money, and you really have no education for what to do with it. Players are better about it now. But we didn't talk about money back then, and we didn't have much of a plan for taking care of it.

It changed in the 1990s, when free agency came about and people started making six-figures plus. It became real money. You could make $200,000 or $250,000 in the 1980s. It was good money, but it wasn't put-you-away money. If you played three or four years and put $500,000 away, that wasn't going to retire you. If you put $5 million away, you could be close to retirement.

Everybody who knows Cortez Kennedy knows how much money he has in the bank because he was always so proud of his investment ability that he would announce it. "I've got $11 million." Now I think it's up to $17 million—"I've got $17 million."

He's not trying to brag. He's just trying to let everybody know that he's been smart with his money.

And that has never been as common as you might think—now or when we were trooping up to Mickey Loomis's office to get our checks in the 1980s.

chapter 12
Game Day

The old Kingdome was also known as "the Blue Thunder Dome" for how loud it would get during big games.
Courtesy AP/Wide World Photos

The Blue Thunder Dome

Everyone asks me (Moyer): what was the loudest game you've ever played in? It was a Monday night game against the Raiders in the Kingdome. It was so loud we had to tape the ear holes of our helmets. They were doing the decibel comparison on TV, and it went up to 136 decibels or something—the equivalent of a jet engine or rock concert. It literally hurt. You had to put your fingers in your ears. And they had like nine waves going at once. It was nonstop. It was nuts.

We were in warmups an hour or so before the game, and the stadium was already three-quarters full. As we clapped, the whole crowd started to clap with us. It still gives me goose bumps. It just kept going until the beat kind of got screwed up. It was just the most unbelievable moment. You just thought, "There's no crowd like that anywhere." An hour before the game, the crowd was completely focused on our team, clapping with us in beat, and it was loud.

Other NFL fans come to the game to have fun; Seahawks fans come to the game to go to work. They know they're part of something special, and that fuels their enthusiasm. Most fans just follow their team, but Seahawks fans actually have some ownership in the team's success. When the crowd is that loud, it takes away the advantage the offense gets from knowing the snap count. The offense has to go on movement just like the defense, so it is definitely a huge advantage for the home defense. One guy who is well aware of that is Seahawks CEO Tod Leiweke, and that's why he always pumps up the Seahawks fans and talks about what an asset they are.

Usually, it would take a couple of series to get into the flow of the game and get the adrenaline pumping pretty steadily. Once you got a couple of hits, you would start feeling like you were in that zone. But the crowd noise at the Kingdome was like an instant injection of adrenaline into your body. And you could feel in the zone immediately.

Every team had stories about coming up here. They were always kind of nervous and timid coming in. Guys like Howie Long and Lawrence Taylor seemed so ordinary in the Kingdome. John Elway looked like he just wanted to leave without getting hurt.

The Kingdome was such a huge advantage that it made an average player good and a good player great. It gave an advantage to undersized guys with quickness. Rufus Porter and Jacob Green were great pass rushers for us, and in the Kingdome they were almost unstoppable. Green once said the Dome fans were responsible for as many as 50 of his 116 career sacks. Porter also credited the fans for many of his 41 sacks.

Sometimes I (Moyer) felt like I was a spectator. The crowd was going wild, the defensive line was getting after the quarterback, and I would sit back and watch it and think, "Wow, this is a good feeling. It's a really great game to watch." There's not a better feeling in the world playing and watching your defense play in a zone. The Kingdome helped us do that a lot.

"We loved it," former defensive tackle Joe Nash said. "But as difficult as it was for the offense, it still at times was a detriment to our defense. We had to use hand signals. George Dyer used to let Jake [Green], Jeff [Bryant], and I do our own thing in the middle. Half the time we couldn't hear what the other guy was saying."

A perfect example of how the crowd noise could hurt us: In 1986 we were playing the New York Giants in the Kingdome. I (Moyer) was about four yards from the line of scrimmage, and I heard cornerback Terry Taylor barking something at me. And I was thinking, "Doesn't he know you can't hear anything in the Kingdome?" He kept barking, and I waved him off, as if to say, "Whatever."

The next thing I knew, Phil Simms dropped back and launched a pass to a guy for a touchdown. Taylor had come up into the flat, and the guy was wide open. After the play, he came over and was yelling at me, "Damnit, I said, 'Cleo!'" Which meant that the corner rolled up and the safety played deep.

I told him, "You never make the call. I make the call. I was four yards from the line of scrimmage. At what point do you think I got your call?"

We almost went at it right there on the sideline, but Kenny Easley broke us up. Thank God we won that game (17–12).

You could be inches from a teammate and screaming at the top of your lungs and yet hear absolutely nothing. It made it really difficult for me because I (Wyman) was calling the huddle and making adjustments. We had to use hand signals, run up and tap people on the butt. There were a lot of things we couldn't do. It did hamper us a little bit.

But what more than made up for it was the adrenaline rush. After I made a sack against the Raiders in a Monday night game in 1988, the crowd was going nuts. As I ran off of the field, I felt like I was floating on air. The hard hits were that way, too. It was almost as if it were so noisy, you couldn't feel anything.

At one point in that game, the Raiders were called for illegal procedure five times in a row because the crowd was so loud the L.A. players couldn't hear the quarterback.

Dave Krieg loved it, too—most of the time. "It was such a great benefit," he said. "You'd be on the sideline, and the place would be deafening. It would send chills down your spine. On the flip side, they would boo very loud when something went wrong, and that would send chills down your spine the other way."

In 1989 the owners passed a rule that would penalize the home team if their fans were so loud that the opposing offense could not call their plays.

The referees would warn us that we were going to get penalized. But there was nothing we could do. It was futile. You couldn't stop the crowd.

This isn't a knock on Qwest Field, but we never had to ask the Kingdome crowd to get louder. We actually had to wave the crowd to be quiet. But it never worked. It just exacerbated the situation.

Today's crowd gets fired up, too. And they help the defense as much as the Kingdome crowds did—it's reflected in the number of false starts the fans have helped force at Qwest. The feel of Qwest Field and the sound is so much more natural. Maybe it's the fans being on top of you. I've been to every stadium, and there's no atmosphere like Qwest Field.

And they're just carrying on that great tradition of noise that started in the Dome back in the 1980s.

Oh, Crap!

Does a person go to work if he or she has a splitting headache, a 103-degree temperature, the chills, and diarrhea? Well, you certainly do if you are an NFL player.

The day of a big game in 1989, I came down with the symptoms I just described. My first thought was, "Oh, no. Not today. Any day, just not today." I knew I was very sick, but I also knew I was definitely not going to miss the biggest game of the year thus far. I didn't mention my condition to anyone. It's not good to show any sign of weakness on game day to anyone, especially not to one of your coaches.

So I did my best to ignore it and proceeded with my usual pregame preparation as if there were nothing wrong with me. It's amazing what your body can handle when there is a lot at stake. I was actually feeling pretty good by the time we were halfway through warmups. As a matter of fact, I was feeling perfectly fine until just before kickoff.

As always, we said the Lord's Prayer just before heading out onto the field. So we collectively hit a knee and started to pray. By the time we got to "Give us this day our daily bread," my stomach let out an audible groan (the sound of my "daily bread" churning in my upset stomach).

I realized I was going to have to go before I headed out onto the field. There was no way I was going to spend the next three hours worrying whether or not I was going to crap my pants in front of 65,000 people. Not to mention the millions at home who would watch me crap my pants in slow motion.

As soon as we said, "Amen," I sprang to my feet and bolted past my teammates on a hasty path to the nearest bathroom stall. It's tough enough for a big guy to sit in one of those stalls without shoulder pads, but with pads? Forget it.

When I finally squeezed my way down on to the porcelain, something occurred to me: the starting defense was to be announced to those 65,000 people whether I was there or not, and that was going to take place in about two and a half minutes.

Sure enough, as I sat wedged into one of the least dignified places a person can be stuck, I heard the stadium announcer bellow, "At linebacker, from Stanford University...David Wyman." You could almost hear the sound of a huge question mark rising from the crowd as *no one* ran onto the field. I sat there thinking, "Every person in this stadium is turning to the person next to them and saying, 'He's probably in the locker room taking a crap.'"

To complicate things further, I looked down and, to my horror, saw that there was no toilet paper! Everyone, including the entire support staff, had left for the field, and I was all alone. I started yelling out for anyone who could hear. Eventually, a janitor walked in and casually tossed me a roll from the next stall and went back about his business.

I finished up *my* business and ran into the training room to grab a roll of tape. That way I could run onto the field busily taping my wrists or fingers so it would look like I had some last-minute taping to do. "Yeah, that's it folks. You see, it was very important that I stay in the locker room to tape my wrists. That's why I missed my introduction, not because I was taking a crap."

And that would have worked had there not been a three-foot-long toilet-paper tail following me onto the field.

When You Gotta Go, You Stay

Tom Catlin was a tough, competitive SOB.

One game, he had the flu and needed to unload. We kept telling him, "Just go to the locker room and take care of it, Coach." But there was no way he was leaving the field during the game.

So he had the sideline attendants stuff towels into his pants, and he sat there on the sideline bench and crapped his pants in front of 60,000 people while giving us the defensive plays. We were trying to pay attention to what he was saying, but you could see guys kind of backing away.

It was a testament to his dedication.

Players would do the same thing. For most players, there was no way you would risk missing a single play. The thought of leaving the field for even one play was incomprehensible. So some guys would just relieve themselves right there, whether it was peeing their pants or defecating. I've heard stories of guys having to throw away shoes after the game because they smelled of urine.

So Tom Catlin just did what any dedicated football guy would do.

Turf Talk

Once the game started, even the most civil, well-mannered guy could be turned into a foul-mouthed jerk.

You get Tourette's syndrome on the field, and things come out of your mouth that don't normally come out of your mouth. I (Moyer) would pray before every game: "God, keep my mouth shut." Because, when the game was over, I would feel so bad about all the things I had said.

When we played a barnburner against the Raiders at the Kingdome on Monday night in 1988, we were determined not to let Bo Jackson run over us as he had in that 1987 game, when he ran for more than 200 yards. My way of negating him was to get in his head, and I cussed him out after every play.

"Get your sorry butt back to the huddle, you blankety-blank!" I verbally harassed him the whole game, using every cuss word you can imagine. With about two minutes left in the game, it looked like we were going to win—we were up 35–27—and after one more time of my saying, "Get your bleeping butt back to the huddle," Jackson looked at me and stuttered a little bit as he said, "F-f-f*ck you, Moyer."

Two things hit me. One, I realized I had gotten to him. I had never gotten to anybody like that before, and he was frustrated. Then the next realization was I felt bad.

It bothered me so much after the game. I later told my son the story, and he said I need to write Bo Jackson a letter and ask for forgiveness, and I plan to do it before my life is over.

I (Wyman) remember one game in San Diego, this guy was holding me on every play—well, I always thought guys were holding me on *every* play—and I told him to get his hands off me, using more f-words in a short span than you might think possible. I was expecting him to turn around and say, "F*ck you, too, Wyman." And then it would be on.

But he just turned to me and calmly said, "Hey, man, why do I gotta be all that [all the things I called him]?"

He totally disarmed me, and I was so surprised, all I could come up with was, "Okay, I'm sorry....You're not."

We were playing Cleveland, and the refs had called back an interception I (Moyer) had made because they called pass interference on Eugene Robinson. I knew it was a bad call, and I just started chewing on this ref about it. I was in the end zone, the fans were booing, and I gave them the Italian salute. That's when I learned how the Dawg Pound got its reputation; they pelted me with dog biscuits.

Then, as I'm cussing out the officials, the referee said, "Hey, Paul." We had condos in the same complex down in Palm Springs, and he knew me. I was so embarrassed because my mouth was going nonstop.

You had to work yourself up into such a state that it was hard to deprogram yourself after a game and go back to the real world. That's why I (Wyman) loved away games, because you would get on the bus and be around your teammates; it was like a decompression time for six or seven hours until you got home.

But when you had to go home to your family or be around other people right after the game, it was always very difficult. There were several times when I had to meet family or friends out in the parking lot or hang out with them right after the game ended. Occasionally, someone would make a crack about a play that I blew or mention a time when I got run over, and I would instantly see red...but then have to calm myself down and remember that I was among "civilians."

I loved the demeanor of NFL referees. It's a shame to me when I watch the NBA or MLB games and these umpires and referees get their tender little egos bruised and throw a guy out of a game. The NFL refs are so much tougher and thicker-skinned. I put that thick skin to the test a few times, though.

I was a pretty good double-bumper on the field-goal team. I would hold the inside gap with my body and then at the last second lunge to get the outside rusher. One time against Kansas City, Bennie Thompson had obviously studied my technique on film and was tackling me so I couldn't get to the outside guy. We almost got a field goal blocked because of it, and I went ballistic. He and I exchanged shoves and verbal unpleasantries until side judge Mike Carey (who is now a referee) broke it up.

I went back to the sideline as hot as could be. Right after that I was back on the field in the defensive huddle getting ready to call the defense when Carey came into my huddle and said very casually, "Hey, Dave, what was that all about with Thompson?" There was something about the way he said it and the fact that I was still really upset. All I could get out was, "Get the f*ck out of my huddle! Just get the f*ck out of here!"

He put his hands up in surrender and laughingly said, "Okay, okay, we'll talk later," and backed away. He knew I was ticked off, and he was smart enough to just leave me alone for a while. Later, after I had cooled down, I went over to him and apologized and explained to him what was going on. He told me he'd watch for it; and to this day, he remains my favorite NFL official. You couldn't do that to a major league umpire without being ejected.

There are always so many f-bombs going on, and it gets personal. The referees eventually will walk up to you and say, "One more word out of you, and I'll flag you." And at that point you've got to back off.

They'll take it for a while before they tell you to calm down. The league tells them they are going to be called every name in the book, and they have to take it. The league says, "What you're here to do is call the game. The players are emotional, and you cannot get into it with them."

There are so many judgment rules, especially pass interference. Those calls affect the game and livelihoods. We wanted to pick our battles, but when we did, we were usually pretty fired up about it.

Against Pittsburgh one year, I (Wyman) was getting held on every running play. I was trying to complain to the umpire who stood just behind me, but you only have 30 seconds between plays, and I had to get the call from the sideline and get everyone lined up. So any screaming and complaining was never very articulate or effective. It was mostly swearing and grunting. And all of that screaming can get you winded, which makes it even harder.

When there was finally a break in the action, I had calmed down, so the umpire came up and asked me what was going on.

I said, "It's like the World Wrestling Federation out here! The left guard is literally tackling me to the ground!"

He said, "Okay, I'll watch for it."

I replied sarcastically, "Hell, I'm starting to get used to it."

He smiled and replied, "Oh, now you're just trying to hurt me, Dave."

We both laughed...

And he never did call holding.

Favorite Foes

John Elway: Dave Krieg in a Maserati

John Elway revolutionized the game. He was a big guy who could run and throw the ball. He was like Dave Krieg in a Maserati. Same competitive attitude, always so driven, but his physical attributes were outstanding.

I (Wyman) remember going to a team party my rookie year, and the Broncos were on *Monday Night Football*. Elway would take off running, and everyone would start yelling, "There goes that freak! Look at the freak go!" I didn't know what they were talking about until Joe Nash told me he was called that because of the freakish things he could do. Everyone was in awe of the things he could do, throwing the ball from one side of the field to the other when we thought we had him cornered. As Nash said, he was like Harry Houdini sometimes.

In my first game as a rookie, Fredd Young got dinged up a little, so I went in for a play—I looked like Don Knotts out there with knees knocking and teeth chattering. I was lined up across from Elway, and he looked across the line and winked at me. I remember thinking, "Oh, you son of a bitch! Don't do that to me!" He had such confidence, a swagger knowing he was going to win. He was a great player, a tough guy. You could hit him as hard as you could, and he would get up every time.

The Broncos were the team we loved to hate the most. We always enjoyed playing them. We had played them so much. In 1983 we played them four times—preseason, two regular-season games, playoffs. We knew these guys so well.

The Raiders: A Love-Hate Relationship

I (Wyman) loved playing against the Raiders. I grew up in Northern California, so I was a huge Raiders fan in the 1970s. I loved the mystique of the Silver and Black, but when I got into the NFL, it seemed like they were still trying to hang on to that old image even though they weren't very good. Their players would walk past you on the field and try to give you this hokie little stare-down. It was pathetic. I used to love to beat their butts and then taunt them afterward with, "Commitment to Excellence, my ass!"

chapter 13
Down Time

The bad blood between the Seahawks and Raiders goes back three decades and continues today, as evidenced by this tackle by the Seahawks' Kevin Hobbs against the Raiders' Rod Smart in a 2006 preseason game.
Courtesy AP/Wide World Photos

Guns 'n' Poses

People flip each other so much crap in the locker room, it's ridiculous. Guys get really personal, and if you show the least bit of thin skin, they're just like a pack of wolves. It took me a while to learn that you just had to laugh along with it. If you got sensitive, they would just ride you on whatever it was for the rest of the year.

But there were two rules: you didn't go into someone's playing ability, and you didn't trash wives and girlfriends.

Late one season, one of our offensive starters and a defensive back crossed the line. The starter made a derogatory comment about the defensive back's wife, and the defender insinuated the starter's girlfriend was sleeping around.

I (Wyman) was sitting there getting my ankle taped in the training room, and they were going back and forth with these insults. All of a sudden, the starter got really serious and said, "When I get down off this table, I'm going to kick your ass." The DB quickly disappeared and then came back in there and kept grabbing his crotch and saying there was something wrong. It was very weird.

I went to the locker room, and the starter got off the table and went over to the defensive back, who showed the starter what was in his sweats—a gun. The defender pulled it out, cocked it and said, "What are you gonna do now?"

As I was walking back to the training room to get some more tape, around the corner came the offensive guy, who juked past me and sprinted to the parking lot to "go get his shit." I got in the training room, and one of the trainers told me what had just happened.

In 90 seconds, word had spread all over the building, and everyone was on pins and needles. The fact that this had happened and that there was a guy who may be showing up to practice with a small arsenal was a little unsettling.

In the real world, the police would have been called and someone would have ended up in jail. But one of the weight coaches met the guy in the parking lot and calmed him down, and the whole thing was handled in house.

After things calmed down, everybody started in with the jokes: "Is he in when we go shotgun formation?"

"He missed that play—just couldn't pull the trigger."

You might say the jokes were kind of rapid fire. Bang, bang, bang.

There and Back Again

When the strike was over, I (Wyman) told my agent, "This is ridiculous. I'm never going to play here." He encouraged me to go directly to Chuck Knox and ask him for a trade. Given that I was a rookie and also extremely intimidated by Chuck, it was a difficult thing to do. But I walked into his office and said, "Chuck, I'd really like to be traded somewhere else where I could play. I think I could be a starter just about anywhere else."

We had Brian Bosworth, Fredd Young, Keith Butler, Bruce Scholtz, Tony Woods, M.L. Johnson, Greg Gaines, and Sam Merriman. There were so many linebackers that I was the odd man out in Seattle. Chuck was surprisingly calm about it, as if he knew it was coming.

The trade deadline was at 1:00 PM the following Tuesday. I went and played golf in the morning with Merriman and teammate Roland Barbay, then called my agent. His secretary told me a trade had not happened. I was a little disappointed, but then I got a call from Sandy Gregory of the Seahawks. She gave me my flight information—a one-way ticket to San Francisco.

The next day, on page 7 of the Seattle paper, there was a blurb that I had been traded to the 49ers. In the Bay Area, where I had spent my college career at Stanford, the front page of the *Examiner* read: "Niners Get Wyman." I was thrilled.

In order for the trade to be finalized, I had to pass a physical the next day. Talk about a stupid, naïve rookie. During the physical, 49ers doctors asked if I had anything that was bothering me. I had struggled throughout camp with my left shoulder—if I extended my arms to take on a block, it would pop out and hurt so bad that I would almost pass out. So I gladly volunteered to the doctors, "Yeah, you know what, my shoulder pops out of socket sometimes."

After the physical, I went back to the 49ers facility, slipped on my No. 59 jersey, and headed out to the field for my first practice. I got about 10 steps onto the field when somebody from the front office said, "Hey, where are you going? It's not official. Come back in here." So I went back inside, and that was the closest I ever got to being a 49er. By that night, the deal was off.

Back in Seattle, I was walking through Sea-Tac Airport, totally dejected. I had my head down and was trudging out of the terminal to get a cab home. Out of the corner of my eye, I could see a guy walking next to me in lock step. It was Sam Merriman. He had heard the whole thing and, 36 hours after he had dropped me off at the airport, he was picking me up again. That was Sam Merriman—a great teammate and friend.

I was traded for second- and fourth-round picks. The 49ers said I needed surgery on my shoulder. They told the Seahawks, "We're going to do surgery on his shoulder. If he can't play in the 1988 season, we want it to be a second and sixth for him." Seahawks president Mike McCormack, who didn't want to do the whole thing in the first place, just said, "Send him back."

Another point of naïveté on my part—all I had to do was get on the phone and tell Mike, "I'm not coming back. Just make it work." But I just shrugged and said, "Oh, okay, I guess I'm going back to Seattle."

And the next week I was running down on kickoffs against Green Bay.

Howard's Place

We had this old retired Seattle cop named Howard who volunteered to work at the team facility. He always had beer, so we would go to the laundry room off the locker room after practice and sit and have a few beers and relax. He put up a sign, calling it "Howard's Place."

You never wanted to get hurt because you would have to stay after practice and go through treatment and all that stuff. Dave Krieg would stick around because he wanted a drinking buddy. He would go back and fill beer up in Gatorade cups and break out the cribbage board. He would keep you company because he knew you couldn't go anywhere, and he always wanted to compete. So we would enjoy a few cold ones while playing cribbage and sitting in the hot tub. Dave made post-practice training room bearable because he would keep you occupied.

Dave also was the only guy I (Moyer) know who could go out on the field and practice with chew in his mouth. Most of us would carry our can of chew in our socks in practice or throw it on the sideline.

I remember being so mad at Dave. He'd be on the sideline bugging everybody, and he'd have a chew. Practice was like a resort for him. We were out there sweating, busting our butts. And he was out there relaxing.

Silk Stalker

Once I (Moyer) went to training camp, I didn't want a girlfriend. Well, the girl I was dating one year had relatives in Spokane, and she moved in with them while we were in camp.

I didn't call her because I told her, "Look, I'm in camp."

She got upset and decided to send a male Stripper Gram to our lunch one day. He started to sing "Happy Birthday," and I said, "You will die in about 10 seconds if you don't leave."

He said, "Well, I got paid to do this."

And I said, "You've been paid. Get out."

I called her up, and she said, "Well, if you had called me…"

chapter 14
Seattle's Best

Jim Zorn, shown here in the early 1980s, was one of the first great players on the Seahawks.

All-Time Teams

Dave Wyman's All-Time Seahawks Team

- **QB** Dave Hasselbeck: I'm going to have to wimp out on this one and say Dave Hasselbeck or Matt Krieg. If I had played with Matt, it would probably be a no-brainer, but Dave will always be my quarterback.
- **RB** Shaun Alexander: He can't catch, won't block, and leaves yards on the table, but he definitely was the most productive back in team history.
- **FB** John L. Williams: He was such an offensive threat, but Mack Strong sure makes it a tough decision.
- **WR** Steve Largent: "Yoda" was truly the master. How did a slow little white guy get defensive backs so turned around?
- **WR** Brian Blades: Tough guy, great teammate.
- **TE** Mike Tice: Herman Munster. A great blocker, but there was a button on his hand that made his legs fold up every time he caught a ball.
- **LT** Walter Jones: When it's all said and done, he'll be the best of all time.
- **LG** Steve Hutchinson: See above. He's a revolutionary player. His value will continue to play out in Minnesota.
- **C** Robbie Tobeck: Very underrated. He made only one Pro Bowl, but should have made more. From the neck up, the best center of his era.
- **RG** Bryan Millard: Even though he did the "Pro Bowl Pout" every year.
- **RT** Steve August: Maybe he couldn't hang with the modern players, but he was a consistent starter for a lot of years.
- **DE** Jacob Green: 116 sacks for minus-753 yards, 28 forced fumbles, 17 fumble recoveries, and four touchdowns. And those weren't the best things about him. It was his leadership.

DT	Joe Nash: I can still see him holding guards so they couldn't get upfield and block me. Thanks, Joe!
DT	Cortez Kennedy: It's impossible to get 14 sacks coming from the inside. But it's the things he did when he wasn't making a play that made him special.
DE	Michael Sinclair: Where did this guy come from? Quietly a distant second to Jake with 73.5 sacks.
LB	Terry Wooden: Very underrated. And you need to know only one thing about him: Tom Catlin loved him.
LB	Keith Butler: My mentor. More than 800 tackles. Another one of Catlin's favorites.
LB	Lofa Tatupu: So smart and instinctive. And you can see his love for the game in everything he does.
SS	Kenny Easley: I love hearing Moyer talk about this guy. He was the most serious guy I ever met. Fierce, intimidating.
FS	Eugene Robinson: I couldn't believe someone that skinny could hit so hard.
CB	Dave Brown: An instinctive playmaker who was a coach on the field. He lives on in Lofa's play.
CB	Marcus Trufant: I believe his best seasons are still to come. He's the best tackling corner I've ever seen.
Punter	Who cares?
Kicker	Josh Brown: Even though he's a traitor and signed with the Rams, I liked watching him run down and make tackles on kickoffs.
ST	Fredd Young: Spectacular hits on kickoffs. He told me he once hit a kick returner so hard that the guy's legs flipped up and hit Fredd right between the legs. He stood up and celebrated with one fist over his head and the other holding his balls.
Coach	Chuck Knox: I had no idea what a great head coach he was at the time. He taught me lot about life.

Paul Moyer's All-Time Seahawks Team

QB Matt Hasselbeck: This is tough. I love Dave Krieg, and if you asked me who I'd pick for one game we had to win, I'd probably give the slight nod to Dave. But when you go to a Super Bowl, the team can't win without you, you've broken just about every passing record, had the best five-year run in Seahawks history, and have been arguably a top-five QB in the NFL over the past five years, Matt gets the title.

RB Curt Warner: Curt created holes. He didn't have a great offensive line. If Curt could have had the 2005 offensive line, he would have broken every record in NFL history, and no one would have broken it. He was that good and quick early in his career. The knee injury and AstroTurf ruined a potential Hall of Fame career. No. 37 (Shaun Alexander) had better stats, but he wasn't a better running back or teammate.

FB John L. Williams: Best all-around fullback in Seahawks history and one of the most underrated in the NFL during his career. He could win a game blocking, catching, or running the ball.

WR Steve Largent: Hall of Famer was the greatest wide receiver ever up until his retirement. A few have passed him since, but no one did what he could do with such a lack of speed (4.7-second 40) and height (under 6').

WR Brian Blades: This was a tough one over Joey Galloway and Darrell Jackson, but Brian gets it because of what he was as a teammate and because he was successful even though he didn't have a complementary wide receiver on the other side. He was the ultimate gamer. You always knew he would bring his A game.

LT Walter Jones: One of the greatest big-man athletes ever to play on the offensive side of the ball. Arguably the best player in Seahawks history. Long arms and great, great feet.

LG   Steve Hutchinson: Best pulling left guard I've ever seen. Nasty attitude and a guy who wanted to destroy his opponent. He had a defensive player's mentality.

C   Robbie Tobeck: Great athlete, just look at his high school basketball highlight reel. Very smart too. Underrated in the NFL but not in Seattle.

RG   Chris Gray: You don't start 16 years and break most consecutive games played in Seahawks history without getting the nod. He was not flashy, but he deserves the nod. He played back in the 1990s, when steroids were rumored, but you never hear anyone mention his name. He never complained; he just got the job done.

RT   Steve August: This was a tough pick, too. But August was the first good one the Seahawks had on the right side. He was scrappy and smart, the type of player coaches love to coach.

TE   Itula Mili: I know this is a reach, but he had a few good years (112 catches from 2002 to 2004) when we really needed a tight end to step up and be a threat. I'd have given it to Mike Tice, but longevity alone wasn't enough, and he just wasn't very good (sorry Tice; you know I love ya).

DE   Jacob Green: One of the best and most consistent leaders in Seahawks history. Seahawks career leader in sacks. Gave everything he had on every play.

DT   Joe Nash: Saved more games blocking kicks and freeing up LBs to be the heroes than anyone. Did all the little things—fake injuries, take on double teams, anything to help us win. Plus he had longevity—a franchise-record 218 games played.

DT   Cortez Kennedy: A certain Hall of Famer and the best of all time at his position for one year—1992, when he was NFL Defensive Player of the Year.

DE   Michael Sinclair: Got the most out of his ability. He was durable. Just another great Seahawk no one knew of coming out of college.

LB	Rufus Porter: This one might draw a "huh?" from some people, but Rufus was one of the most feared pass rushers in the league during his time, especially in the Kingdome. Rufus was one of the reasons the defensive flinch rule was changed. He was a great special-teamer with a great motor. You could tell he loved to play the game.
LB	Lofa Tatupu: Quick feet lead to being a great tackler, and Lofa has very quick feet for a thumper. He's also a natural leader and instinctive player who gets the most out of his body.
LB	Keith Butler: Chad Brown was on my list, but injuries and lack of tackles took him off. Keith was the second-smartest football player I've ever played with (John Harris was first). Keith was the rock of the defense in the early/mid-1980s. He led the team in tackles every year. He also was a team leader; no one on our team messed with Keith once we were between the white lines.
CB	Dave Brown: My life mentor. He was 6'2" and 200 pounds, which was big a cornerback then. He was a Pro Bowler in 1984 and is still the franchise's all-time interception leader. He was a fantastic athlete with great hands and feet. No one worked harder than Dave on or off the field. He was the most respected man on our team.
CB	Marcus Trufant: This was a tough one over Shawn Springs, but Marcus is a better playmaker. He has exceptionally quick feet. He's small compared to some corners in the league, but he makes up for it with his toughness. I think he's the best all-around corner in the league—he tackles, covers, and makes plays.
SS	Kenny Easley: This wasn't even close. Kenny was the greatest safety to ever play the game. He was smart, tall, fast, athletic, mean, and ferocious on the football field. Offenses changed their game plans because of Kenny.
FS	Eugene Robinson: He was a Dave Brown protégé. Dave mentored Eugene on work habits both on and off the

field. Eugene became a playmaker in the early 1990s once he gained confidence. He was benched in 1989 but fought his way back and became a Pro Bowler in 1992 and '93 for the Seahawks. He was a resilient, sure tackler who led the team in tackles for many years, which is hard to do as a free safety.

ST Fredd Young: He killed people on kickoffs. He almost decapitated the Raiders' Dokie Williams on national TV. Fredd also was a great pass rusher and punt-blocker. He probably was the greatest playmaker in Seahawks history for the amount of opportunities he had.

Punter Who cares? We could put best ball boy in this category (Randy Mueller). Rick Tuten actually looked like a football player, so he's the guy.

Kicker Who cares? Part II. Efren Herrera at least made it fun. Josh Brown got a small vote, but he sings backup vocals to Craig Terrill and played eight-man football in high school. Enough said.

Coach Mike Holmgren: Tough call between Mike and Chuck Knox. Both were great coaches for the Seahawks, but Mike gets the edge because of the Super Bowl appearance. Chuck did more with less talent, but Mike has taken this team to five straight playoffs.

The Ring of Honor

Steve Largent—Wide Receiver, No. 80, Inducted 1989

Obtained just before the Seahawks' first season, Largent was the best receiver of his generation. A seven-time Pro Bowl player, Largent set six major NFL receiving records—receptions (819), consecutive games with a reception (177), receiving yards (13,089), receiving touchdowns (100), seasons with 50 or more receptions (10), and seasons with 1,000 receiving yards (eight). He was the first man inducted into the Ring of Honor as the team put him in at halftime of his final game. In 1995 he became the Seahawks' first Hall of Famer when he was inducted on his first ballot.

Moyer: Largent was a consummate professional. He was the hardest worker at improving his craft of anyone I've ever known. He was a gamer who always came up with the big catch. People said he wasn't a great athlete, but he was; he just didn't have a great 40 time or an athletic body. He had incredible body control and balance and was exceptional at coming out of breaks in his routes. I used to call him Houdini because he would trick you into believing he was going one way and then he would go the other. He could beat a double team just as easily as beating single coverage. He came across as mild-mannered but had a nasty competitive streak on the practice field and during games. He also was very humble.

Wyman: I used to marvel over how twisted around he would get defensive backs. There's a great picture of him catching a touchdown, wide open against the Chargers. The San Diego defender in the picture is 10 yards behind him and facing the wrong way. And these were guys who were much better athletes than Largent. With his size and speed, he might not even get invited to the NFL Combine today—what a mistake that would be.

Jim Zorn—Quarterback, No. 10, Inducted 1991

The leader of the early Seahawks offenses, Zorn was NFC Rookie of the Year in 1976 after throwing for a rookie-record 2,571 yards. Zorn started 100 games for the Seahawks and finished with 20,122 passing yards, 107 touchdowns, and 133 interceptions in nine seasons with the team. He was replaced by Dave Krieg midway through the 1983 season.

Moyer: I remember growing up watching him. He wore black shoes, and he was a left-handed QB who could run, which in itself was a rarity. I grew up in Southern California, and the only thing I remembered about the Seahawks was No. 10. He loved to play the game. He was a gym rat. If he could, he would still play. He was a fantastic communicator and great leader.

Wyman: I know Jim more as a coach than as a player. I used to watch him run some of the strangest drills in practice and then watch them come to life on the field on game day. He's a great teacher.

Dave Brown—Cornerback, No. 22, Inducted 1992

Obtained from the Pittsburgh Steelers in the 1976 veteran allocation draft, Brown became one of the Seahawks' best defenders over the next decade. He is still the best cornerback to ever play for the team, holding team records in interceptions (50), interceptions for touchdowns (five), and return yards off interceptions (643). He died in January 2006 after collapsing during a pickup basketball game at Texas Tech University, where he was an assistant coach.

Moyer: Dave was a mentor about life to many people. He was a strong Christian who never wavered in his beliefs and a hard worker who loved to work one-on-one drills against Steve Largent. He had a smooth, effortless backpedal with great hands. I'll never forget his two interceptions for touchdowns against Kansas City in 1984; his last one was his best as he grabbed it with one hand. He strived to be the best in everything he did, I mean everything: the best husband, father, player, and coach. He was a very humble leader.

Wyman: Coaches tell defensive backs all the time, "When the ball goes up in the air, think of it as your ball." Dave didn't need to be told that. He probably had better hands than Largent. But it was his smarts that made him such a spectacular player.

Pete Gross—Broadcaster, Inducted 1992

Gross was the Seahawks' radio play-by-play voice for 17 seasons. Gross, known for his high-pitched call of "Touchdown Seahawks," announced every game from the inaugural 1976 season through 1991. In 1992, as he battled terminal cancer, he was inducted into the Ring of Honor before the Seahawks' Monday night game against the Denver Broncos. The Seahawks won the game in overtime—one of their two wins that season—and Gross died two days later.

Moyer: Pete was so gracious. He didn't know how good he was at what he did. And he was beloved and respected by everyone. When I was coaching in 1992, I had a chance to sit with him on the airplane on his last road game with us. I knew he wasn't going to be with us much longer. I was so honored when they moved him up to sit next to me. I asked him a few questions, and for the next few hours he told me as much as he could about his life. It was like someone reading you the greatest book in the world.

Wyman: My most vivid memory of Pete was a few weeks before he died. He was at the team facility to interview me before a game. He was entirely yellow from the jaundice caused by his illness. He was the sweetest guy in the world, and all during the interview, all I could think was: "Oh, Pete...I'm so sorry."

Curt Warner—Running back, No. 28, Inducted 1994

The number-three pick in the stellar 1983 draft, Warner made his presence known immediately by rushing for a team-record 1,449 yards and 13 touchdowns and being named to the Pro Bowl. After missing almost all of 1984 with a knee injury, Warner rebounded with four excellent seasons before the knee eventually ended his career prematurely. A three-time Pro Bowl running back, Warner ended his seven-year Seattle career with a team-record 6,705 rushing yards and 55 rushing touchdowns.

Moyer: C.W. was a gifted athlete who had a burning desire to succeed in football and in life. He could stop on a dime and be at full speed three steps later. He was a very focused, disciplined person, with great morals and humility. And he was my best friend.

Wyman: Curt was such an interesting character. He loved to laugh, and his personality didn't seem to go with his playing ability. He was too humble. I can still hear that high-pitched voice saying, "What's up, Wy-monster?"

Jacob Green—Defensive end, No. 79, Inducted 1995

A first-round pick in 1980, Green is the Seahawks' career sack king, having accumulated 116 during a 12-year career. He also holds the club record with 28 forced fumbles, including a team-record seven during the 1985 season. Green's 178 games played are fourth in franchise history, while his 176 games started are second.

Moyer: Speed kills, and Jacob had speed for a big man. I remember Jacob returning a fumble 79 yards against the Jets in 1985. He started out fast, but the piano on his back made for an entertaining last 10 yards. He was the emotional leader of the team, and he wasn't afraid to show his emotion. He didn't judge anybody, but he held everyone accountable, and he always had his teammate's back covered. Everyone who had a chance to play with Jacob Green loved to play with him.

Wyman: I always think of the time once before a game when he said he was going to get three sacks. And then he went out and got them. It's like the hitter who gets up to bat and points to the fence and then whacks a home run. When Jake spoke, people listened. He was a great leader.

Kenny Easley—Safety, No. 45, Inducted 2002

Easley, the team's top pick in 1981, quickly became the most dominant safety in the NFL. He was named the NFL Defensive Player of the Year in 1984, when he tied a team record with 10 interceptions and scored twice. He went to five Pro Bowls during a seven-year career that tragically ended with a life-threatening kidney disease. The three-time All-Pro finished with 32 interceptions.

Moyer: Kenny was a special athlete who could do anything. He wanted to be the best at what he did both on the field and in the business world. He dominated the league in 1984 with 10 interceptions and devastating tackles. At the time, he was the greatest safety to ever play the game. He was a leader by example. I wanted and tried to emulate him, but that was an impossible feat.

Wyman: Kenny was the most fearsome and serious player I ever met. He had an air about him much like Chuck Knox. You just knew you were supposed to respect the guy.

Dave Krieg—Quarterback, No. 17, Inducted 2004

The undrafted free agent out of Milton College took over as the Seahawks starter in 1983 and proceeded to lead the Seahawks to the playoffs four times. He was named to the Pro Bowl three times in his 12 seasons with the Seahawks, and his career numbers (which include seven more seasons with five other teams) rank him among the top 11 quarterbacks in NFL history: 261 touchdown passes (ninth), 5,311 attempts (10th), 3,105 completions (10th), and 38,147 passing yards (11th).

Moyer: Dave was a competitor, a gamer, and a very hard worker. He was the Man from Milton, one of the great rags-to-riches stories in the NFL—a free agent who seemingly had no chance from a school that doesn't exist anymore. He went on to play 19 years and throw 261 TD passes. If I had to choose a player for just one game that we had to win, I'd take Dave every time.

Wyman: Dave was always trying to find a way to win. He was a true warrior, and the example he set on the field was something I learned from greatly.

Chuck Knox—Coach, Inducted 2005

Knox arrived in Seattle in 1983 and immediately turned the Seahawks into a playoff contender, taking them to the AFC title game in 1983 and back to the playoffs three more times in his nine seasons. He finished as the winningest coach in franchise history (80–63), although he was surpassed by Mike Holmgren (82–62) in 2007.

Moyer: A master of motivation, Chuck knew how to prepare his team better than any coach I've ever played for. He was a great talent evaluator, and everything he did had a reason behind it. He had great attention to detail.

Wyman: Chuck was the best head coach I ever had. He possessed a perfect blend of football knowledge and leadership. I wish I could have played for Chuck my entire career.

Cortez Kennedy—Defensive Tackle, No. 96, Inducted 2006

The team's first pick in 1990, Kennedy quickly became the most dominant defensive tackle in the NFL. In 1992 he joined Easley as one of only two Seahawks to be named NFL Defensive Player of the Year, as Kennedy finished with 14 sacks, an astounding 92 tackles, and four forced fumbles. Kennedy was named to a team-record eight Pro Bowls during his 11-year career.

Moyer: Not a mean bone in his body, yet Tez destroyed anyone in his path during the 1992 season. He was the most dominant player in the NFL in the early 1990s. If they made a cartoon after his character, every child would love him. Tez proved nice guys can finish first.

Wyman: The most lovable guy I ever met. He was probably the best teammate I ever had, too. In 1992 there were times I would be in the middle of a play, and I'd catch myself watching Cortez in action and think, "I can't believe he just did that!"